U0483702

符号中国 SIGNS OF CHINA

中国棋艺

ART OF CHINESE BOARD GAMES

"符号中国"编写组 ◎ 编著

中央民族大学出版社
China Minzu University Press

图书在版编目(CIP)数据

中国棋艺：汉文、英文 / "符号中国"编写组编著. —北京：
中央民族大学出版社,2024.3
（符号中国）
ISBN 978-7-5660-2286-8

Ⅰ.①中⋯ Ⅱ.①符⋯ Ⅲ.①棋类运动—介绍—中国—汉、英 Ⅳ.①G891

中国国家版本馆CIP数据核字（2024）第016883号

符号中国：中国棋艺 ART OF CHINESE BOARD GAMES

编　　著	"符号中国"编写组
策划编辑	沙　平
责任编辑	满福玺
英文指导	李瑞清
英文编辑	邱　械
美术编辑	曹　娜　郑亚超　洪　涛
出版发行	中央民族大学出版社
	北京市海淀区中关村南大街27号　邮编：100081
	电话：（010）68472815（发行部）　传真：（010）68933757（发行部）
	（010）68932218（总编室）　　　　（010）68932447（办公室）
经 销 者	全国各地新华书店
印 刷 厂	北京兴星伟业印刷有限公司
开　　本	787 mm×1092 mm 1/16　印张：8.75
字　　数	113千字
版　　次	2024年3月第1版　2024年3月第1次印刷
书　　号	ISBN 978-7-5660-2286-8
定　　价	58.00元

版权所有　侵权必究

"符号中国"丛书编委会

唐兰东　巴哈提　杨国华　孟靖朝　赵秀琴

本册编写者

房　明

前言 Preface

　　下棋，古称"博弈"，是中国人传统文化生活的重要组成部分。中国的围棋、象棋等棋类经过几千年的发展，早已超越了娱乐消遣的范畴，成为一种特殊的艺术形式，具有丰富的文化内涵，并且间接影响着中国人的道德观念、审美趣味和思维方式。在看似

　　Playing board games, also called the Game (*Boyi*) in ancient times, is an important part of Chinese people's culture and life. The game of Go and Chinese chess with thousands of years' development, have been endowed with more significant meaning than its entertainment function and become a unique form of art with rich and profound cultural connotation which

简单的方格棋盘和棋子之间，在一来一往的落子声中，传统的哲学、兵法、诗词、书画共冶一炉，中国文人的机智、豁达、风雅、恬淡展露无遗。

　　本书详细介绍了围棋、象棋、六博、双陆等中国传统棋艺的发展历程、棋具规则及其与中国文化密不可分的关系，希望帮助读者了解中国棋艺，并且通过棋艺进一步领略中国传统文化。

exerts indirect influence on Chinese people's moral concepts, aesthetic interest and way of thinking. Within the sound of moving pieces, the simple square board and chess pieces re ect the mixed essences of traditional philosophies, military strategies, poetry, Chinese painting and calligraphy and reveal the wisdom, generosity, elegance and inner peace of Chinese literati.

　　This book introduces the origin and development of Go, Chinese chess, Liubo, Shuanglu and other traditional board games, as well as the sets and rules, which have close relationship with Chinese culture. Hope it can assist the audience to gain a general understanding on Chinese board games and also take a further step in knowing and feeling traditional Chinese culture.

目 录 Contents

围棋
Go 001

围棋的起源与发展
Origin and Development of Go 002

围棋棋具与规则
Sets and Rules of Go 032

围棋与中国文化
Go and Chinese Culture 040

中国象棋
Chinese Chess 065

中国象棋的源流
Origin of Chinese Chess 066

象棋的棋具与规则
Sets and Rules of Chinese Chess 077

象棋与传统诗画
Chinese Chess and Traditional Chinese
Poetry and Painting 089

其他棋艺
Other Board Games 095

六博
Liubo 096

塞戏
Saixi 103

弹棋
Tanqi 105

双陆
Shuanglu 109

蒙古象棋
Mongolian Chess 119

藏棋
Tibetan Board Games 122

鄂伦春围棋
Oroqen Board Game 125

围棋
Go

　　围棋是中国古代文人、士大夫最喜爱的娱乐竞技活动之一，同时也是历史最为悠久的一种棋戏。围棋将竞技与艺术修养、人生体悟融为一体，不仅有助于发展人的智力、锻炼人的意志，并且可以培养出机动灵活的战略和战术意识，因而几千年来长盛不衰。

Go, one of the favorite entertainment and competition games of ancient Chinese literati, was the oldest board game in history. It has integrated athletic skills with aesthetic taste and life experience of its players, which helps them to develop wits and will and teaches them practical strategies, and thus it has been popular for thousands of years.

> 围棋的起源与发展

围棋在古代称为"弈",在整个古代棋类中可以说是棋之鼻祖,相传已有4000多年的历史。自古以来,关于围棋的起源就有着多种说法。在记载先秦时期(前221以前)历史的《世本》中,古人将围棋的发明归功于远古五帝之一的尧帝。西晋时(265—316)的张华在其所撰的《博物志》中也说:"舜以子商均愚,故作围棋以教之。"(舜帝因其儿子商均愚笨,所以发明了围棋来开发他的智力。)尧和舜都是传说中的人物,造围棋之说并不可信,而且围棋是一项复杂的竞技活动,不可能是某一个人创制的。它应当是在一段较长的历史时期内逐渐发展而来的,是众人智慧的结晶。

> Origin and Development of Go

Go was known as "*Yi*" in ancient China. It dates back to over 4,000 years ago and is regarded as the primogenitor of board games. There are various sayings about the origin of Go. According to the *Shiben* (*Books of Lineages*), a history text written before the Qin Dynasty (before the 221 B.C.), it was the legendary ancient Emperor Yao who invented it. Nevertheless, according to the *Bowu Zhi* (*Records of the Investigations of Things*) written by the scholar Zhang Hua of the Western Jin Dynasty (265-316), "Go was invented by Shun to enlighten his less intelligent son Shang". However, it is not sensible to enshrine Yao and Shun as the inventors of Go, because they are imaginary figures from ancient mythology. As a complex adversarial game, Go may not have been created by

传说中的尧舜时期处于中国原始社会的末期，那个时代的数学、天文学、阴阳学和军事知识都有了很大的发展，为围棋的诞生打下了基础。甘肃永昌出土过一批原始社会末期的陶罐，其中不少罐身上都绘有黑色、红色甚至彩色的条纹图案，线条均匀，纵横交错，格子齐整，很像现在的棋盘，考古学家称之为"棋盘纹图案"。可以推想，a single mind, but gradually developed through collective wisdom in a long historical period.

The legendary emperors Yao and Shun might have lived during the last years of China's primitive society when mathematics, astronomy, Yin and Yang theory, and military tactics made great progress, which laid the foundation for the invention of Go. Several pottery jars made in the late primitive society were unearthed from Yongchang County of Gansu Province. Many of them were painted with black, red or colorful strip patterns with evenly-distributed crossing lines which form neat checks and thus resemble a modern Go board. Such patterns have been named as the "board pattern" by archaeologists. Hence, we may infer that Go had its early form in primitive society.

• 舜帝像
舜为远古时代的部落联盟首领，古代贤明君主的代表之一，受尧帝的禅让而即位。

Portrait of Emperor Shun
Shun was the chief of tribes' union in ancient times and was regarded as one of the best sage rulers. He was enthroned after his predecessor Yao's abdication.

• 马家窑文化彩陶罐（新石器时代）
Painted Clay Jar from Majiayao Culture
(Neolithic Age, 10,000-4,000 years ago)

围棋在原始社会已具雏形，纵横交错的棋盘已基本形成。

  春秋战国时期，围棋已在社会上广泛流传了。在记录春秋时期历史的史书《左传》中记载了这样一件事。公元前559年，卫国国君卫献公因骄横无道，被卫国大夫孙文子和宁惠子驱逐出国。后来，宁惠子临死前后悔，吩咐儿子把卫献公迎回国来。孙文子批评道："弈者举棋不定，不胜其耦，而况置君而弗定乎？"就是说，下棋的人拿着棋子犹豫不决，就不能战胜对手，更何

During the Spring and Autumn Period (770 B.C.-476 B.C.) and the Warring States Period (475 B.C.-221 B.C.), Go had been widely circulated in the society. According to *Zuo Zhuan* (*Commentary on the Spring and Autumn Annals*), Duke Weixian, the ruler of the State of Wei was expelled by scholar-bureaucrats Sun Wenzi and Ning Huizi in 559 B.C. due to his arrogant and violent behaviors. Subsequently, when Ning Huizi was dying, he regretted for what he had done to the king and commanded his son to bring Duke Weixian back to the State of Wei. However, Sun Wenzi criticized Ning Huizi's decision by saying: "If the player of Go is indecisive, he will lose the game. How can you lack of a decisive mind for such an important issue about our king?" It means that it is impossible for the player of Go to win the game if he cannot decide the next step without hesitation. As for more important matters, like whether we shall have the king back, we need to be more decisive. Sun Wenzi's using Go as a metaphor to explain the harm of indecisiveness in political issues indicates that Go was commonly seen in the society at that time. The first famous Go player in written historic records was named Yi

Qiu. According to the Confucian classics *Mengzi* (*Works of Mencius*) written in the Warring States Period (475 B.C.-221 B.C.), "Yi Qiu is a player of Go whose fame has spread to every state". His skills of Go was so good that the book *Yidan Ping* (*Commentary on Famous Players of Go*) regarded him as the "originator" of Go.

During the Qin Dynasty and the Western Han Dynasty (221 B.C.-8 A.D.), there were few historic records about Go except for *Xijing Zaji* (*Miscellany of the Western Capital*), a book recording anecdotes happened in the Western Han Dynasty (206 B.C.-25 A.D.). It mentioned that Du Ling who lived in the early Western Han Dynasty was the best player of Go at that time. He regarded playing Go as the most important thing in

- 《四皓弈棋图》谢时臣（明）

  "四皓"指的是秦代的四位隐士，为避危乱，逃离秦都咸阳，隐居在陕西商山。后代画家经常以商山四皓隐居的故事为题材进行绘画创作。

  Four Hermits Playing Go, by Xie Shichen (Ming Dynasty, 1368-1644)

  "Four Hermits" refers to four of the hermits who lived in the Qin Dynasty (221 B.C.-206 B.C.). They escaped from the capital city Xianyang to Shangshan Mountain of Shaanxi to avoid death threat. Their story in Shangshan Mountain is frequently featured in paintings by subsequent artists.

弈秋与弟子

战国初期，有个人特别擅长下围棋，堪称当时第一高手。他因棋艺高超而出名，所以人们都叫他"弈秋"。据《孟子》一书的记载，由于弈秋棋术高明，有很多年轻人想拜他为师，向他学习棋艺。弈秋收了两个学生。一个学生诚心学艺，听先生讲解时十分专心；而另一个学生只是慕名而来，虽拜在弈秋门下，但在弈秋讲棋时却经常心不在焉，老是朝窗外看，一心想着鸿鹄鸟什么时候飞来，好张弓搭箭射它两只。这样一来，两个学生虽然同拜一个老师，但前者学有所成，而后者却始终未能领悟棋中真谛。《孟子》书中讲这个故事，就是为了告诫人们，做任何事都要专心致志，才能有所成就。

Yi Qiu and His Apprentices

During the early Warring States Period, there was a man who was so good at playing Go that he had no competitor. He was renowned for his skills of Go and known as "Yi Qiu". According to *Mengzi* (*The Works of Mencius*), due to Yi Qiu's fame, many young people wished to learn how to play Go from him. Nevertheless, he only had two apprentices. One came for Yi Qiu's skills and always concentrated in class, and the other came for Yi Qiu's fame and didn't pay enough attention in class. He was so lucky to be Yi Qiu's apprentice, but he often looked outside of window and wondered when the swans would fly pass so he could use his bow to shoot some. Therefore, both of the apprentices were taught by Yi Qiu, but only the dedicated student became a good player of Go and the absent-minded one was never able to know the quintessence of Go. This story tells us the importance of dedication in success.

况对待国君这样的大事呢？孙文子用"举棋不定"这种围棋术语来比喻政治上的优柔寡断，说明围棋活动在当时社会上已经在一定范围内流行。第一位见于文字的围棋高手是战国时齐国的弈秋。战国时期儒家经典《孟子》一书中载："弈秋，通国之善弈者也。"弈秋是当时各国

life. When someone taunted him wasting his time on Go, he replied: "If I master the quintessence of Go, I can make up for the areas even Confucius failed to cover." As an ancient literati, he dared to say something like this about Confucius, which showed that he indeed treated Go seriously and possibly as a type of art and science. Besides, Go also prevailed

都知晓的国手，棋艺高超，品评历代棋手棋事的明代著作《弈旦评》推崇他为围棋"鼻祖"。

秦代到西汉年间（前221—公元8），有关围棋活动的记载较少，但收录西汉时遗闻轶事的笔记小说集《西京杂记》中曾提到，西汉初年的杜陵"善弈棋，为天下第一人"。他棋艺高强，好棋如命。有人讥笑他在下棋上花工夫是浪费时间，他却这样回答："我精通了围棋之道，可以弥补孔夫子之不足。"一个古代文人竟敢说这样的话，可见他确实是把围棋当作一种艺术和学问来研究的。汉代宫中盛行围棋。据《西京

in the imperial court during the Han Dynasty (206 B.C.-220 A.D.). *Xijing Zaji* (*Miscellany of the Western Capital*) mentioned that the founder of the Han Dynasty Liu Bang would play Go with his beloved concubine Madame Qi on the fourth day of the eighth month every year. Gradually, playing Go on that day became a tradition in the imperial court. Aside from Du Ling, Liu Qu and Chen Zhu were also famous for their skills of Go. It was said that the Emperor Xuan of the Han Dynasty was pleased by Chen Zhu's performance when they played Go together and appointed him as the Prefect of Taiyuan later. In the Eastern Han Dynasty (25-220), Go became more

- 陶制围棋罐和围棋子（汉）
Clay Go Stones and Clay Bowls for the Stones (Han Dynasty, 206 B.C.-220 A.D.)

国手

在古代，精通某种技能（如医道、棋艺等）而在当时达到该领域最高水平的人，被称为"国手"。这个称呼尤以棋坛使用更多。《唐诗纪事》中记载，诗人裴说的《棋》诗中有"人心无算处,国手有输时"的名句。时至今日，人们仍习惯用"国手"二字形容棋艺高超的棋士。

National Champion

In ancient times, people who mastered certain skills (such as medical knowledge, playing Go, etc.) and reached the highest level in the field were known as "national champion". This title was often given to players of Go. According to *Tangshi Jishi (Collection of Criticism on Poets and Poetry of the Tang Dynasty)*, there was a famous verse from the poem *Go* written by the poet Pei Yue that "no one can work out everything, because even the national champion loses his game sometimes". Up to the present, "national champion" is still used to describe grand masters of Go.

杂记》记载，每年八月四日这一天，汉高祖刘邦的爱妃戚夫人总要陪刘邦下围棋。渐渐地，在八月四日这一天，下围棋成了汉宫中的风俗。西汉时以棋扬名的人还有刘去和陈逐。据说，陈逐因陪汉宣帝下棋，讨得天子欢心，后来还得了太原太守的官职。到了东汉时，围棋更为盛行。中国第一部断代体通史《汉书》的作者班固还著有《弈旨》，这是历史上第一篇专门论述围棋理论的文章。东汉末年，围棋进入了一个大发展的时

prevalent. Ban Gu, the compiler of *Han Shu (Book of Han)* and the originator of the format for dynastic history, wrote a paper called *Yi Zhi (The Essence of Go)*, which was the first paper on the theories of Go. The late Eastern Han Dynasty (25-220) witnessed great development of Go and many excellent players were recorded in history. In the year 1952, a square stone Go board with four feet and 17 by 17 grids on its surface were unearthed from the No. 1 tomb of the Eastern Han Dynasty in Wangdu, Hebei Province

期，涌现出大批优秀的棋手。1952年，考古工作者于河北望都一号东汉墓中发现了一件石质围棋盘，呈正方形，盘下有四足，局面纵横各17道。这件棋盘的发现为汉魏时期围棋盘的形制提供了形象的实物资料。

三国时期（220—280），围棋又达到了一个新的阶段，成为当时最受欢迎的游艺活动。爱好下棋的人越来越多，从帝王、文人士大夫到各阶层民众。围棋流行的区域也

- **曹操像**
曹操（155—220），字孟德，三国时期曹魏政权的缔造者，著名的政治家、军事家、文学家。

Portrait of Cao Cao
Cao Cao (155-220), courtesy name Meng De, was the creator of the Kingdom of Wei during the Three Kingdoms Period (220-280). He was a famous statesman, warlord and litterateur.

by archaeologists. The discovery of this board provided important evidence for the format of Go board during the Han Dynasty and the Three Kingdoms Period (220-280).

During the Three Kingdoms Period (220-280), Go reached its new stage and became the most popular recreational activities. Go had more and more players from all walks of life, including the emperors, the literati and commoners. It also spread to wider areas from the Central Plains and Yellow River basin to the south of the Yangtze River.

Go flourished in the northern areas under the regime of the Kingdom of Wei (220-280), because it was the favorite game of the ruler Cao Cao's family. Cao Cao loved Go and reached a high level. He even played against some of the famous players of Go. Two of his sons including Cao Pi (Emperor Wen of the Kingdom of Wei), Cao Zhang (Prince of Rencheng) also enjoyed playing Go. Besides, Wang Can, one of the seven famous prodigies of Jian'an Period (196-220), was also known for his skills of Go apart from his fame in poetry. It was said that one day Wang Can was watching others playing Go, but somehow the game was messed up. He rearranged

更为广泛，从中原地区和黄河流域逐渐扩大到了江南地区。

曹魏政权控制下的北方地区，围棋活动由于曹操家族的爱好和提倡而蓬勃发展。曹操本人不仅爱好围棋，而且棋艺水平较高，曾与当时的围棋高手对局。曹操的两个儿子魏文帝曹丕和任城王曹彰也喜好围棋。而当时"建安七子"之一的王粲，除了以诗赋闻名于世外，同时也是个围棋高手。据说一次王粲看人下棋，棋局乱了，王粲凭着记忆就重新摆出了原来的棋局。旁人不敢相信，用布把复盘的棋局盖起来，请王粲再摆一遍。王粲第二次摆出了打乱前的棋局，对照之下一子不错。在《弈旦评》一书中，王粲被誉为"弈中神人"。

蜀汉政权的建立者刘备占据蜀地后，他的大批将领和官员中不乏围棋的爱好者，其中以丞相诸葛亮和名臣费祎最为著名。这些围棋爱好者的活动推动了蜀地围棋的发展。

在东吴，围棋活动更是风行。东吴政权的奠基者孙策、大将陆逊等人都是围棋的爱好者。据说孙策常在与臣子对弈时商讨军国大事，

the pieces and restored the last scenario of the game. The bystanders could not believe their eyes, and used a cloth to cover the Go board and asked Can to arrange the pieces again on another board. Can rearranged the pieces again and the comparison between the two boards proved that he didn't make any mistakes. He was praised as the God of Go by the book *Yidan Ping* (*Commentary on Famous Players of Go*).

After Liu Bei came to Sichuan and established the Kingdom of Shu-Han (221-263), he brought with him a large number of generals and officials and many of them were fond of Go, which

• 青瓷熏炉（三国吴）
Celadon Censer (Kingdom of Wu in the Three Kingdoms Period, 222-280)

• 东吴大将陆逊像
Portrait of General Lu Xun from the Kingdom of Wu

而陆逊在军情紧急时也能弈棋如常。东吴棋风很盛，甚至常有官员因下棋而耽误公事。为此，东吴太子孙和命一个叫韦曜的文人写了篇《博弈论》，批评这些下棋误事的人。围棋风行到这种程度，名手自然越来越多，精彩的对局也随之出现。此后，经典的对局慢慢被人记录下来，变成棋谱，一代一代流传下来。

魏晋时期（220—420），政局虽然动荡不定，但帝王皇室和士族

helped the development of Go in Sichuan. The most famous players among them were the Prime Minister Zhuge Liang and the renowned court official Fei Yi.

In the Kingdom of Wu (222-280), playing Go also prevailed there. Its enthusiastic followers included Sun Ce—the founder of the Kingdom of Wu and the general Lu Xun, etc. It was said that Sun Ce and his court officials could discuss important issues while playing the Go, while Lu Xun could play Go as good as usual even when he faced emergent situations in war. However, as playing Go was so popular in the Kingdom of Wu, sometimes the court officials delayed their business for it. To criticize these addicts, Sun He, the crown prince of Wu, asked a scholar named Wei Yao to write the article *Boyilun* (*The Theory of Game*). Many good players of Go, as well as their nip and tuck scenarios emerged due to the popularity of this game. Some of the classic scenarios in the game was recorded as tutorials of Go and passed on to later generations.

Political situations during the Three Kingdoms Period and the Western Jin and Eastern Jin dynasties were volatile, but this did not stop the kings, the royal families, and other aristocracy to live a

晋武帝司马炎像
Portrait of Sima Yan, Emperor Wu of the Western Jin Dynasty (265-316)

阶层仍过着优游奢侈的生活，士人们崇尚清谈，追求享乐，文学、史学、宗教、书法、绘画、雕刻等在这一时期都有很大的发展。围棋也得到帝王和士族的重视，在朝野上下十分风行。西晋的建立者晋武帝司马炎就非常喜好围棋。《晋书·杜预传》载，公元280年，将军杜预向晋武帝启请讨伐吴国。他将表章送至宫中时，晋武帝正在同棋手张华下棋。晋武帝原本不想立即

luxurious life. They advocated talking shop and enjoyed pursuit of pleasure, and thus literature, history, religion, calligraphy, painting, and carving gained rapid development at that time. Besides, as the rulers and aristocracy also liked playing Go, it became very popular in the imperial court. Sima Yan, founder of the Western Jin Dynasty (265-317) known as the Emperor Wu was fond of Go. According to the *Biography of Du Yu* in *Jin Shu* (*The Book of the Jin Dynasty*), in the year 280 A.D. General Du Yu came to plea for declaring a war against the Kingdom of Wu. When he arrived with his memorial tablet, Emperor Wu was playing Go with Zhang Hua and did not show any intention to have a war with the Kingdom of Wu right away. Nevertheless, as Zhang Hua supported Du Yu's proposal, he moved the board aside and suggested the Emperor to fight against the State of Wu immediately. Finally, Emperor Wu agreed to Du Yu's proposal. Go was even more popular among aristocratic scholars. For instance, celebrity scholars who were masters of Go including Cai Hong, Cao Shu, and Yin Zhongkan, and Yang Tao, as well as Ruan Ji and Wang Rong were known as the "Seven Sages of the Bamboo Grove".

伐吴，但张华支持杜预的意见，把棋盘推开，主张马上出兵，晋武帝这才同意。在当时的士族文人中，围棋更是广受青睐，名士蔡洪、曹摅、殷仲堪、羊陶及"竹林七贤"中的阮籍、王戎等都是围棋高手。东晋时期，朝中最为显赫的王、谢两大家族，包括拥立东晋元帝司马睿的王导、成功指挥淝水之战的谢安，以及许多族中子弟都爱棋成痴，水平极高，东晋的棋风之盛可见一斑。

当时的围棋除继承了以前斗智、娱乐的传统外，陶情怡性的艺术成分明显增强，人们在临局对弈时更重视感情的抒发与交流，文人则更将下围棋作为修身养性之道。围棋从此又被赋予"手谈"的雅称。

In the Eastern Jin Dynasty (317-420), many young men from the two most influential families in the imperial court loved Go and could play it extremely well. Some of them were related with Wang Dao who contributed to the enthronement of Sima Rui as the first Emperor of the Eastern Jin Dynasty, and others were from the family of Xie An who commanded the army and achieved victory in the Battle of Fei Shui. Their devotion to Go revealed its prevalence at that time.

In addition to its nature as a game for competition and entertainment, Go included more artistic features during this period. Players paid more attention to expressing and exchanging feelings. Literati even regarded playing Go as a way of self-cultivation. Hence, playing Go was also known as "hand communication".

- 青釉褐彩刻花莲瓣纹盘口壶（东晋）
Brown-glazed Celadon Jar with Broad Mouth and Eversion Rim and Carved with Lotus Petal Pattern (Eastern Jin Dynasty, 317-420)

阮籍与围棋

"竹林七贤"是魏晋文人中很有代表性的人物,他们崇尚老庄虚无之学,优游于竹间林下,放旷不羁,大多喜爱围棋,而且有许多惊世骇俗之举。"七贤"中的阮籍(210—263)是著名的文学家。他为逃避司马氏集团的迫害,常醉酒佯狂,不拘礼教。《晋书·阮籍传》中说他是个孝子。他母亲去世时,他正与人下围棋。消息传来,对局者请求罢棋,而阮籍却坚持要一决胜负。一局终了,他"饮酒二斗,举声一号,吐血数升"。

Ruan Ji and Go

"Seven Sages of the Bamboo Grove" were representatives of the literati lived during the Three Kingdoms Period (220-280) and the Western Jin Dynasty and Eastern Jin Dynasty (265-420). They advocated of the nothingness theory of Laozi and Zhuangzi. They also travelled around, and enjoyed a bohemian lifestyle. Most of them loved playing Go and were known for their shocking behaviors. One of them was Ruan Ji (210-263), a famous litterateur. To avoid the persecution of the Sima family, he often got drunk, pretended to be mad, and ignored the ethical codes. According to the *Biography of Ruan Ji* in *Jin Shu* (*History from the Jin Dynasty*), when his mother died, he was playing Go and his counterpart asked for pausing the game, but he refused. At the end of the game, he drank some alcohol, cried out loudly, and vomited lots of blood.

- 《竹林七贤》年画(清)
New Year Picture: *Seven Sages of the Bamboo Grove* (Qing Dynasty, 1616-1911)

南北朝时期（420—589），围棋继两晋蓬勃发展的势头，地位更高，出现了盛极一时的局面。南朝共历宋、齐、梁、陈四朝，历代帝王大都爱好并提倡围棋，如宋文帝刘义隆、齐高帝萧道成、梁武帝萧衍都嗜好下棋，并且格外宠爱棋艺水平高的臣子。他们以棋设官，建立"棋品"制度，对有一定水平的棋士授予与棋艺相当的"品格"（等级）。这样一来，围棋的地位大大提高，逐渐成为朝廷中带有礼仪性质的活动项目，甚至成了一些人加官晋爵的阶梯。另一方面，围棋的艺术价值也进一步得到承认，

The Southern and Northern dynasties (420-589) witnessed Go's further upgrade of status and then reached its peak of development after its booming momentum during the Western Jin and Eastern Jin dynasties. All emperors of the Southern Dynasties including the Song of the Southern dynasties (420-479), the Qi of the Southern dynasties (479-502), the Liang of the Southern dynasties (502-557), and the Chen of the Southern dynasties (557-589) were addicted to playing Go and they favored court officials who could play Go well. They used the skills of Go as the criteria to select officials and determine their ranks. Thus, good players of Go would have equivalent official

- **青釉刻花莲瓣纹唾壶（南朝）**
  Celadon Spittoon Carved with Lotus Petal Patterns (Southern Dynasties, 420-589)

王质烂柯

晋朝时有一位叫王质的人，有一天他到信安郡的石室山去打柴。他看到两位老者在溪边的大石上下围棋，于是把砍柴用的斧子放在旁边的地上，驻足观看。看了多时，老者说："你该回家了。"王质起身去拿斧子时，发现斧柄（古称"柯"）已经腐朽了，磨得锋利的斧刃也锈迹斑驳。他回到家里后，发现家乡已经与以前大不一样，乡邻中没人认得他，提起他的事，只有几位老者还有印象，但也都说那是几百年前的事了。原来，王质在石室山打柴时误入仙境，遇到了神仙。仙界一日，人间已是百年。后来，"烂柯"就成为围棋的一个别名，这个故事也常常被人们用来形容人世间的沧桑巨变。唐代诗人刘禹锡的诗中就有"到乡翻似烂柯人"之句，表达了他离开京城二十多年后，人事巨变给他带来恍如隔世的感觉。

Wang Zhi, the Woodcutter and His Rotten Axe Handle

In the Jin Dynasty, there was a man named Wang Zhi. One day, he went to the Stone Chamber Mountain of the Xin'an County to cut firewood. On his way, he saw two old men playing Go on a big stone by the side of the river, so he put down his axe by his side and watched the game. After a while, the old men said: "You should Go home." When Wang Zhi stood up and picked up his axe, he found the handle of the axe was rotten and the sharp blade of the axe rust away. When he returned to his hometown, he found it looked different and none of the fellow villagers could recognize him. When he mentioned about himself, only few old people could have some clues about his story but they said this had happened hundreds of years ago. It turned out that Wang Zhi entered the wonderland of the immortals. One day there equaled to a hundred years on earth. Later, the phrase "rotten axe handle" was used to as an alternative name for Go. Liu Yuxi, a poet lived in the Tang Dynasty (618-907) once wrote that "When I came back, I felt like it were Wang Zhi who returned to his hometown", expressing his feelings towards the capital city, after he had been away for over 20 years and noticed tremendous changes had happened there.

● 《烂柯图》荷叶形瓷盘（宋）
Lotus Leaf-shaped Porcelain Plate with the *Rotten Axe Handle Scene* (Song Dynasty, 960-1279)

白釉瓷围棋盘（隋）
White Porcelain Board of Go (Sui Dynasty, 581-618)

成为与书法、绘画并列的艺术门类。一时之间，上至宗室皇亲、文人、士大夫，下至民间的老弱妇孺、方外隐士，无不以下棋为乐。

唐宋时期（618—1279），社会局面较为稳定，经济和文化都得以繁荣发展，围棋进一步得到普及，对弈之风遍及全国。唐代"棋待诏"制度的实行，是中国围棋发展史上的一个新标志。所谓"棋待诏"，就是唐代翰林院中专门陪同皇帝下棋的专业棋手。当时，供奉内廷的"棋待诏"都是从众多的棋手中经过严格考核后入选的。他们都具有第一流的棋艺，有"国手"之称。唐代著名的棋待诏，有唐玄

ranks. As a result, the status of Go was further upgraded and gradually became an etiquette activity in court, and even a shortcut of getting promotion. Besides, the artistic value of Go was further recognized and became one of the three major artistic types aside from calligraphy and painting. Hence, at that time, everyone loved playing Go, no matter whether they were the royal families, literati, aristocrats, ordinary people of all ages, and hermits.

From Tang Dynasty to Song Dynasty (618-1279), with the stabilization of the society and flourishing economy and culture, playing Go became even more popular around the country. The establishment of the system to select "Imperial Go Attendants" in the Tang Dynasty (618-907) was a new landmark in the development of Go in China. The "Imperial Go Attendant" referred to professional Go players who worked at the Imperial Academy to play Go with the emperors. Back then, all the "Imperial Go Attendants" were selected from numerous players through strict tests. All of them reached the highest level at playing Go and were known as "national champions". Famous Imperial Go Attendants in the Tang Dynasty included Wang Jixin in the reign of Emperor Xuanzong, Wang

宗时的王积薪、唐德宗时的王叔文、唐宣宗时的顾师言及唐信宗时的滑能等。由于"棋待诏"制度的实行，扩大了围棋的影响，也提高了棋手的社会地位。这种制度从唐初至南宋延续了500余年，对中国围棋的发展起了很大的推动作用。

Shuwen in the reign of Emperor Dezong, Gu Shiyan in the reign of Emperor Xuanzong, and Hua Neng in the reign of Emperor Xinzong. Due to the implement of the "Imperial Go Attendant" system, the Go gained greater influence and social status of Go players were improved. This selection system lasted for over 500 years from the early Tang Dynasty to the Southern Song Dynasty, which greatly helped the development of Go in China.

王积薪与"十诀"

　　王积薪是唐代最著名的棋手之一，在唐玄宗开元年间（713—741）成为翰林院的"棋待诏"，经常与玄宗下棋。明代学人王世贞曾评价说："唐之弈，以开元王积薪为首。"据唐人冯贽的《云仙杂记》记载，王积薪每次出游必携带围棋棋具，路上随时与人下棋。公元755年，唐玄宗因"安史之乱"南逃时，王积薪还曾跟随玄宗入蜀，足见他在唐代棋坛擅名之久。晚年时，王积薪总结出《围棋十诀》，对后世影响颇深。

Wang Jixin and His "Ten Secrets for Success in Go"

Wang Jixin was one of the most famous Go players in the Tang Dynasty (618-907). He gained his position as an "Imperial Go Attendant" at the Imperial Academy in the reign of Emperor Xuanzong (713-741) and played Go with the emperor for many times. Wang Shizhen, a scholar of the Ming Dynasty (1368-1644) commented, "the best Go player in the Tang Dynasty was Wang Jixin". According to *Yunxian Zaji* (*Miscellaneous Notes of Yunxian*) written by Feng Zhi of the Tang Dynasty, Wang Jixin would take his Go set with him whenever he travelled so he could play Go with others on the way. Even in the year 755, he followed Xuanzong to escape to Sichuan due to the An-Shi Disturbances, which showed his important status in the Go field of the Tang Dynasty. In his later years, he wrote the book named *Ten Secrets for Success in Go* and left a profound effect on later generations.

王积薪"十诀"
Wang Jixin's "Ten Secrets"

1	不得贪胜 Don't be too obsessed with victory	不要贪图胜利而走过分的棋。 Don't use high-risky strategies due to your desire to win the game.
2	入界宜缓 Be careful before you invade your opponent's territory	打入对方阵势要徐徐图之，不求一击而得逞。 Plan carefully and slowly before invading your opponent's territory and avoid attempting to occupy it with one attack.
3	攻彼顾我 Take the defense consideration while launching an attack	要攻击对方时，要想到己方的安危与发展的全局。 When you launch an attack on your opponent's territory, you need to think about how to defend your own land;
4	弃子争先 Make concession to win the chance to attack	不要因小处纠缠而丧失"先手"的主动。 Make concession to avoid losing the chance to launch attack first.
5	舍小就大 Sacrifice the less valuable stones	行棋面临取舍时，衡量得失后选择价值最大的一步来走。 Before you make your decision, evaluate your lost and gains and pick the best strategy.
6	逢危须弃 Give up in dangerous situations	形势不利时就须放弃，放弃的越早损失越小。 Give up disadvantaged stones in less favorable situations. The earlier you give up, the smaller your lost would be.

7	慎勿轻速 Avoid hastiness	对局时要重视对手，小心谨慎，不要盲目出手行棋。 Never look down upon your opponent. Be careful with each step without any hastiness.
8	动须相应 Keep the big picture in mind	下棋时要有全局观念，局部要和全局呼应配合。 Take the whole board into consideration and make sure local fights coordinate with overall situation.
9	彼强自保 Focus on defense if your opponent has gained the upper hand	在敌方势力较强的区域或阶段，要以忍为上，采取自保措施。 When your opponent has gained the upper hand at the moment or in certain places, you should endure this and focus on defending your own territory.
10	势孤取和 Seek for survival in disadvantageous situation	当己方的棋孤身处于对手势力范围时，应避免交战，先保全自己。 If your stones are circled by the opponent side, you should avoid fighting and seek for chance to survive first.

革新名臣王叔文

王叔文（753—806）是唐德宗时的"棋待诏"，史书记载他不仅以棋艺闻名，而且胸怀大志，满腹经纶。他在宫中长期侍奉太子李诵下棋，有时在李诵面前议论朝政，无不切中要害。李诵见他颇有才能，就把他收为心腹。公元805年，唐德宗驾崩，太子李诵即位，是为顺宗。王叔文被任为翰林学士，又兼充度支盐铁转运副使，掌握财权。在王叔文和著名文人柳宗元、刘禹锡等人的协助下，唐顺宗施行了种种整顿朝政、反对宦官专权的改革措施，史称"永贞革新"。谁知不久唐顺宗病重，在朝中一些旧派官僚的胁迫下退位，革新失败，王叔文被杀害。这次变法革新虽然失败了，但作为一名围棋"国手"，王叔文无疑是值得纪念的人物。

Wang Shuwen, A Famous Reformer

Wang Shuwen (753-806) was an "Imperial Go Attendant" in the reign of Emperor Dezong of the Tang Dynasty (618-907). According to historical records, he was not only renowned for his skills of Go, but also for his ambition, and knowledge. He served Crown Prince Li Song as a Go attendant and showed his talent in politics during their discussion about current affairs. Hence, he became a close associate of the prince. In 805 A.D., Emperor Dezong demised and Li Song was enthroned as Emperor Shunzong. Wang Shuwen was named as imperial scholar at the Imperial Academy and deputy director of finances. With the assistance of him and others like famous literati Liu Zongyuan and Liu Yuxi, Emperor Shunzong carried out several reform policies, in particular he attempted to stripe the control of the powerful eunuchs, known as "Yongzhen Reform". However, Emperor Shunzong became extremely ill later and was forced to abdicate under the threat of conservative court officials, and thus the reform failed and Wan Shuwen was killed. Although his reform was a failure, Wang Shuwen, as a national champion of Go, was definitely one of the most impressive professional players.

- 三彩文官陶俑（唐）
  Three-color Glazed Clay Figurine of A Civil Official (Tang Dynasty, 618-907)

从唐代始，围棋随着中外文化交流的发展，逐渐传出国门。日本遣唐使团将围棋带回国内，很快在日本流传开来，不但涌现了许多围棋名手，而且对棋子、棋盘的制作也非常考究。除了日本，还有朝鲜

With the cultural exchange between China and other countries, Go gradually spread outside China during the Tang Dynasty (618-907). Japan's envoy to China took back Go with them and it became an instant hit there. Japan started having its own good Go players and producing refined Go stones and boards. Aside from Japan, there were other countries on the Korean peninsula, including Paekche, Northern Korean Kingdom, and Silla. According to *Xin Tang Shu* (*The New Annals of the Tang Dynasty*), Yang Jiying, a professional Go player from China had opponents from Silla, which proved that the Go players in Silla reached quite high level.

During the Ming and Qing dynasties, the general public had even higher skills of Go and different schools of Go emerged. There were three most famous schools of Go during the reign of Emperor Zhengde and Emperor Jiajing in the Ming Dynasty, including Yongjia

- 《山弈候约图》佚名（辽）
Waiting for Playing Go with a Friend in the Mountain, by Anonymity (Liao Dynasty, 907-1125)

李泌赋棋

李泌是唐玄宗时期的名臣，据说他从小好学，7岁时就敏捷善赋，才名广播。唐玄宗得知后便命人召他入宫。李泌到时，唐玄宗正在同大诗人张说观棋，于是命张说试一试李泌的才华。张说看看面前的棋局和棋子，让他以"方、圆、动、静"为题作赋，并随口说道："方若棋局，圆若棋子，动若棋生，静若棋死。"李泌脱口答道："方若行义，圆若用智，动若骋材，静若得意。"张说所说句句有棋，道出了围棋的特征，而李泌所说虽不带"棋"字，但句句关合围棋，概括出了弈者下棋时的种种情态。张说听后惊诧不已，恭贺唐玄宗说朝廷又得奇才。玄宗也非常喜爱李泌，赏赐给他许多财物。这个故事也反映了唐代围棋活动的兴盛情况。

Li Bi's Ode to Go

Li Bi was a famous court official in the reign of Emperor Xuanzong. It was said that he was bookish as a kid and he was renowned for his quick mind and talent in poem at the age of seven. When his fame spread to the ear of Emperor Xuanzong, he summoned him to the Palace. When Li Bi arrived, Emperor Xuanzong was watching a Go match with the famous poet Zhang Yue. He asked Zhang Yue to test Li Bi's talent. Thus, with the Go match and Go stones in front of them, Zhang Yue asked Li Bi to make a poem based on "square, round, dynamic, and static", and improvised one first: "As square as the board, as round as the stones, as dynamic as the survival stones, and as static as the dead stones." Li Bi replied: "square represents righteousness; round symbolizes wisdom; moving stones are similar to marching cavalry; and static stones are like victory." Zhang Yue's poem explicitly mentioned about Go and described the features of it; By contrast, none of Li Bi's verses mentioned about Go explicitly, but it described the expressions of the players of Go vividly. After hearing this, Zhang Yue was amazed by Li Bi's talent and he congratulated Emperor Xuanzong for getting a genius once again. Emperor Xuanzong also liked Li Bi and rewarded him with many treasures. This story also reflected the prevalence of Go in the Tang Dynasty (618-907).

半岛上的百济、高丽、新罗。《新唐书》中就记述了唐代围棋高手杨季鹰与新罗棋手对弈的情形，说明当时新罗的围棋已具有一定的水平。

School with Bao Yizhong from Yongjia of Zhejiang Province as the leader, Xin'an School with Cheng Ruliang from Xin'an of Anhui Province as the leader, and Jingshi School with Yan Lun and Li Fu

- 《明皇会棋图》周文矩（五代）

唐玄宗李隆基（685—762），又称唐明皇，公元712—756年在位。史书称他"多艺，尤知音律、善八分书"，所谓"多艺"就包括棋艺。他常同大臣、亲王、后妃一起下棋、观棋。

Emperor Xuanzong Playing Go, by Zhou Wenju (Five Dynasties Period, 907-960)

Li Longji (685—762), also known as Emperor Xuanzong and Emperor Ming of the Tang Dynasty reigned over China between the year 712 to 756. According to history, he was talented and in particular good at music and calligraphy (an evolved small seal style). Playing Go was among one of his many accomplishments. He often played Go with the court officials, his brothers, sons, and consorts, or watched them playing Go.

明清两代（1368—1911），围棋棋艺水平得到了进一步提高，而且棋手流派纷起。明代正德、嘉靖年间，形成了三个著名的围棋流派：一是以浙江永嘉人鲍一中为首的永嘉派；一是以安徽新安人程汝亮为首的新安派；还有就是以北京人颜伦、李釜为首的京师派。这三派风格各异，布局攻守侧重不同。在他们的带动下，民间的围棋竞技活动十分盛行，使得围棋进一步得到普及。随之，一些民间棋艺家编撰的围棋谱也大量涌现，如《适情录》《石室仙机》《三才图会》等，都是颇有价值的著述。

在清代，满族统治者对汉文化

from Beijing as the leaders. These three schools had distinct styles, and focused on different defense and attack strategies. With the leading of them, playing Go was very popular in society. Subsequently, many valuable Go manuals complied by good Go players were written, including *Shi Qing Lu* (*Notes* on *Current Trends*), *Shishi Xianji* (*Secrets in the Stone Cave*), and *Sancai Tuhui* (*Picture Encyclopedia*).

In the Qing Dynasty (1616-1911), as the Manchu rulers were interested in Chinese culture and promoted the development of Go, many good players emerged and the Go circles reached its highly prosperous momentum. In the Late Ming Dynasty and the early Qing Dynasty, the most renowned player of Go

• 《芭蕉美人图》姜隐（明）
Fair Ladies under the Plantain Trees, by Jiang Yin (Ming Dynasty, 1368-1644)

的吸收与提倡，也使围棋游艺活动得到了高度发展，这一时期名手辈出，棋苑空前繁盛。明末清初，享名最盛的围棋国手要数过百龄。过百龄是江苏无锡人，自幼聪慧，深受嗜好围棋的父亲的影响。11岁时，过百龄已精通棋道，与成年人弈棋逢局必胜，转战无锡城而鲜遇对手，被称为"神童"。有位名叫叶向高的学台大官来到无锡，要找一位棋力强的对手同他对局，有人

was Guo Bailing. He was born in Wuxi, Jiangsu Province and was intelligent as a kid, who was influenced by his Go loving father. When Guo Bailing was 11 years old, he mastered the essence of Go and won every game even playing with adults. He seldom met any competitor in Wuxi and thus was known as a child prodigy. Once, a high-ranking education commissioner named Ye Xianggao came to Wuxi and asked for a good player of Go to play the game with him. The young Guo Bailing was recommended to him. Ye Xianggao failed for three times consecutively, which spread Guo Bailing's fame in the south of the Yangtze River. When the famous national champion Lin Fuqing in Beijing got to know Guo Bailing's talent in Go, he challenged him and there was money for the winner as reward. Guo Bailing failed to decline the challenge and attended the competition and won three rounds consecutively. After this event, Guo Bailing's fame spread to the whole country and good players from all over

推荐了年幼的过百龄。交手之下，叶向高连败3局。从此，过百龄名扬江南。在北京声望最高的前辈国手林符卿听说过百龄的棋名，主动向过百龄挑战，还有人拿出银子来作为优胜者的奖赏。过百龄推辞不过，只好应战，结果林符卿连输3局。此战过后，过百龄的名字传遍全国，四方名手都来向他挑战，他一一应战，每战必胜。《无锡县

• 《过氏宗谱》上的过百龄像
Portrait of Guo Bailing in the *Family Tree Compilation with the Surname Guo*

the place challenged him. However, Guo Bailing succeeded to win all the games. *County Annals of Wuxi* once recorded: "Then in several decades, Guo Bailing was invincible across the whole country." Later, he wrote several works about Go including *Guanzi Pu* (*Remaining Stone Manual*), *Sanzi Pu* (*Three Stone Manual*), *Sizi Pu* (*Four Stone Manual*), etc. Among them, *Sizi Pu* (*Four Stone Manual*) has been the most widely read and most influential book.

In the late years of the reign of Emperor Kangxi and the early reign of Emperor Jiaqing, famous Go players Liang Weijin, Cheng Lanru, Fan Xiping, Shi Xiangxia were known as the "Four Great Go Players". Fan Xiping (1709-1769) learned to play Go in a young age and became famous in his hometown when he was 13 years old. When he was 16 years old, he started traveling around the Songjiang River areas and defeated other famous players of Go, which spread his fame in the country and made him a national champion. Fan Xiping came to Beijing at his 20 and defeated almost all the famous masters and earned his reputation rapidly. Many high-ranking officials paid him to play Go with them and enjoyed the games. Fan Xiping was

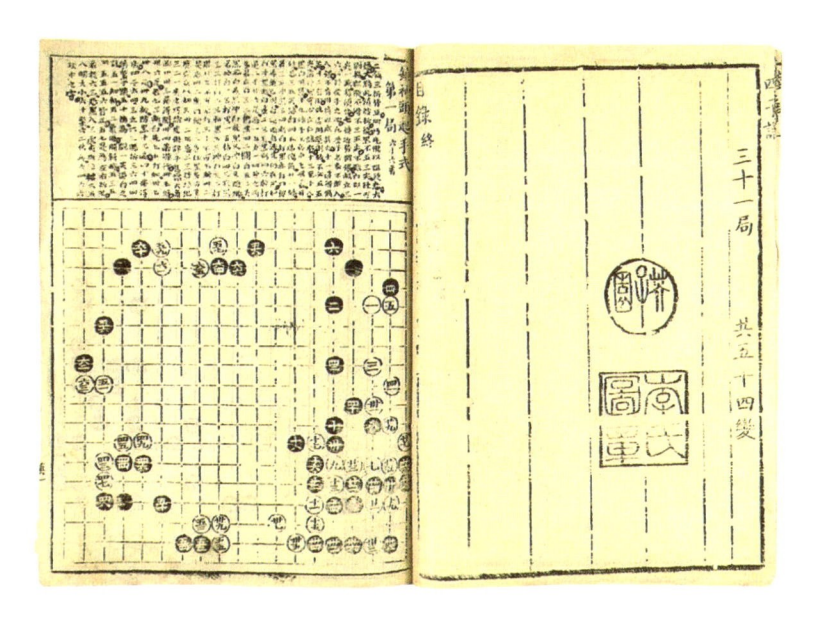

• 过百龄《四子谱》书影
Book Cover of Guo Bailing's *Sizi Pu* (*Four Stone Manual*)

志》中写道："因是数十年，天下之弈者以无锡过百龄为宗。"过百龄的著述世传有《官子谱》《三子谱》《四子谱》等，其中《四子谱》流传既广，影响也深。

康熙末到嘉庆初年，棋坛名家梁魏今、程兰如、范西屏、施襄夏被合称为"四大家"。范西屏（1709—1769）幼年学棋，13岁就在家乡一带崭露头角，16岁起在松江地区游历，屡胜名家，成为国手。20余岁时，范西屏来到京

a great-hearted man and had a deft style of playing Go. At that time, Shi Xiangxia was his only rival. Different from the deftness of Fan Xiping, Shi Xiangxia was prudent. In the fourth year of the reign of Emperor Qianlong (1739), they played Go in Pinghu Lake area (also known as Danghu Lake). They played ten rounds and presented many magnificent situations, which reached the highest level of Go at that time.

After the middle of the Qing Dynasty, Go met its comedown.

师，迎战各地围棋名手，几乎战无不胜，很快名驰全国，不少大官争着拿银子请强手与范西屏较量，以此为乐。范西屏性情豪放不羁，他的棋风也是落子敏捷，潇洒飘逸。范西屏在当时棋坛中罕逢敌手，能与他抗衡的只有施襄夏一人。范西屏下棋轻灵多变，施襄夏稳健持重，二人曾于乾隆四年（1739）

During the reign of Emperor Jiaqing and Emperor Daoguang to the break of the Opium Wars, China suffered great economic depression and social unrest, so the popularity of Go waned. By contrast, in the meantime Go in Japan was booming and Japanese Go players gradually performed better than Chinese Go players. During the Minguo Period (1912-1949), it was trendy to learn to play Go in Japan and thus the players reached higher level than the ones in the late Qing Dynasty. The most famous masters of Go was Wu Qingyuan, who was born in a literati family of Fuzhou City, Fujian Province in 1914 and then moved to Beijing with his family. He showed his talent in Go in his childhood and became a family Go tutor of the Northern Warlord Duan Qirui at the age of eleven. He defeated many famous Go players, and was known as a Go prodigy. In 1928, the fourteen-year-old Wu Qingyuan went to Japan to learn how to play Go and became a professional Go player. In 1939, he defeated

• 范西屏《桃花泉棋谱》书影
Book Cover of Fan Xiping's *Go Manuel from the Peach-blossom Spring*

在浙江平湖（别称当湖）对局。两人先后共下10局，棋局异彩纷呈，可以说达到了当时围棋技艺的最高水平。

　　清朝中叶以后，中国围棋界逐渐后继乏人。从嘉庆、道光直至鸦片战争前后，经济萧条，社会动荡，围棋活动也呈现滑坡的趋势。当中国围棋衰落之时，日本的围棋活动正蓬勃兴起，而且水平已逐渐超过了中国。民国时期，中国棋界掀起了一股学习日本棋艺的新风，围棋水平比清末有所提高。当时最为著名的围棋大师，要数吴清源。吴清源1914年出生于福建省福州市的名门望族，后举家迁入北京。他幼年时就在围棋上表现出过人的天分，11岁时就成为北洋军阀段祺瑞

Japan's seven best players of Go and won "10 rounds of Go", and even lowered the professional rank of his opponents. His astonishing achievements amazed the Go circles in Japan. He was regarded as the best player of Go and opened the "Wu Qingyuan Era". Nevertheless,

- 《孝钦后弈棋图轴》（清）
  这幅作品描绘了孝钦后（慈禧太后）在兰卉绽放的皇家园林中与咸丰皇帝对弈的情景。
  Empress Xiaoqin Playing Go (Qing Dynasty, 1616-1911)
  This painting depicted that Empress Xiaoqin (Empress Dowager Cixi) was playing Go with Emperor Xianfeng in the royal orchid garden.

门下的棋客，与许多当时围棋高手对局，成绩斐然，被称为"围棋神童"。1928年，14岁的吴清源东渡日本继续学棋，并就此开始了职业棋手的生涯。1939年起，吴清源在十次"十番棋"中，战胜了全日本最顶尖的七位超级棋士，并把对手打到降级，取得了空前的战绩，震动日本棋坛，被尊为围棋界首屈一指的实力派棋手，也开创了围棋的"吴清源时代"。真正奠定吴清源

his great achievement was proposing and practicing "New Layouts of Go". In Wu Qingyuan's era, Go in Japan had developed for about 400 years and formed fixed rules. However, young Wu Qingyuan broke the rules and created new layouts, which played important roles in the development of Go theories. In general, due to the social unrest and wars in Minguo Period, it was hard to make a living, let alone to play Go, so China lagged behind in the development

- **清代的围棋桌**
  Go Board (Qing Dynasty, 1616-1911)

• 青花瓷《童子下棋图》盆（清）81279
Blue-and-white Porcelain Plate Painted with *Children Playing Go* (Qing Dynasty, 1616-1911)

of Go compared with other countries.

After the establishment of the People's Republic of China in 1949, Go gained further development. After 1956, Go became a national athletic sports and many famous players of Go emerged, including Chen Zude, Nie Weiping, Ma Xiaochun, Cao Dayun, and Chang Hao, ect.

在棋坛地位的，还是他所提出并身体力行的"新布局法"。在吴清源时代，日本围棋积四百年之传统，形成了许多对于棋道的铁律，而年轻的吴清源突破成规，开创新布局法，为围棋理论的发展起了举足轻重的作用。总体来说，民国时期由于时局动荡，战乱不断，民生艰难，中国围棋与世界先进水平仍有很大的差距。

1949年中华人民共和国成立后，围棋得到了新的发展。从1956年起，围棋被正式定为国家开展的体育运动项目。此后涌现出许多新的围棋名家，如陈祖德、聂卫平、马晓春、曹大元、常昊等。

• 吴清源（图片提供：CFP）
Portrait of Wu Qingyuan

> 围棋棋具与规则

围棋的棋具是棋盘和棋子。

现在的围棋盘面有纵横各19条等距离、垂直交叉的平行线，共构成19×19=361个交叉点。在盘面上标有9个小圆点，称为"星位"，中央的星位又称"天元"。早期的棋盘道数较少。1977年在内蒙古一座辽代古墓中出土了一张围棋方桌，桌上所画的棋局纵横13道，是

> Sets and Rules of Go

Standard Go sets include the board and stones.

The board is marked with 19 parallel horizontal lines and 19 parallel vertical lines, which formed 361 intersections. There are also nine dots on the board, known as the "stars". The point in the center is also known as *Tianyuan* (the central star). Initially, there were fewer lines on the board. In 1977, a Go board with 13 parallel horizontal lines and 13

• 紫砂围棋罐
Purple Sand Go Bowls

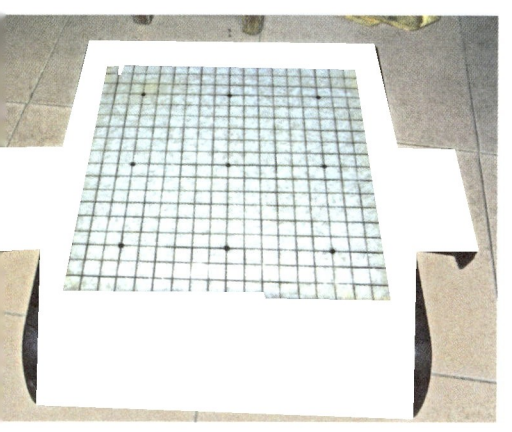

• 木制棋盘
Wooden Go Board

目前所见道数最少的棋局。研究者认为，13道的棋盘是西汉甚至春秋战国以前所通行的围棋制式。在东汉以至三国时期，通行的棋盘为17道。大约在魏晋时期，19道围棋在南方开始流行，到南北朝时，19道围棋逐渐占据主要地位，通行于大江南北，成为标准的围棋制式。

围棋的棋子分为黑、白两色，早期棋子数目根据棋盘道数的多少而变化，17道棋盘共要289子，现在的19道棋盘共需361子，黑子181个，白子180个。棋子呈圆形，中国围棋一般使用一面平一面凸的棋子，而日本围棋的棋子则为两面凸起形。

parallel vertical lines was unearthed from an ancient tomb of the Liao Dynasty (907-1125) in Inner Mongolia. This board had the fewest number of lines that has never seen. According to researchers, the 13-grid board was used before the Spring and Autumn Period (770 B.C.-476 B.C.) and the Warring States Period (475 B.C.-221 B.C.). During the Eastern Han Dynasty (25-220) and the Three Kingdom Period (220-280), the 17-grid board was more popular. Around the period of Three Kingdoms Period (220-280), Western Jin Dynasty and Eastern Jin Dynasty (265-420), the 19-grid board started gaining popularity in the south. In the Southern and Northern dynasties (420-589), the 19-grid board gradually took the upper hand and became more popular, which formed the standard format of Go later.

Go stones are either in black or white. Initially, the number of Go stones depended on the number of lines on the board. As for 17-grid board, 289 stones were needed, while 19-grid board needed 361 stones, including 181 black stones and 180 white stones. The Go stones are round. Chinese stones have a single convex, while Japanese ones have double-convex.

● 红白玛瑙围棋子（元）
Red and White Agate Stones (Yuan Dynasty, 1206-1368)

在材质和制作方面，最早的棋盘和棋子多为木制，也有石制的。魏晋时出现了玉石制成的棋盘和棋子，只限于皇室贵族使用。隋唐五代时，帝王和文人为追求高雅的围棋情趣，对棋具十分讲究，玉石棋具已十分普遍，此外还出现了许多用罕见材料制作的棋具。日本奈良正仓院至今保存着一件紫檀木棋盘，是唐朝皇帝的赠品，棋盘两边还有盛放棋奁的小屉，制作精美，装饰华丽。《云仙杂记》中还提到，当时有富贵人家以紫檀木心和龙脑香做成黑白棋子，以碎金镶嵌于棋盘之上，极尽奢华。

As for materials, early Go board and stones were made of either wood or stone. Jade stones and board was exclusively used by royal families and aristocracy in the Three Kingdoms Period, Western Jin and Eastern Jin dynasties. In the Sui, Tang, and the Five dynasties, the royal families and literati pursued elegance of Go, so they preferred exquisite sets of Go. Thus, it was common to see jade stones and boards. Besides, there was Go equipment made of rare materials. In Shoso-in of Nara City in Japan, there has been a Go board made of red sandal wood, which was a gift from an emperor of the Tang Dynasty. On the two sides of the Go board, there are two exquisite small drawers with glamorous decorations. According to *Yunxian Zaji (Miscellaneous Notes of Yunxian)*, some rich families owned Go stones that were made of red sandal wood and borneol wood and Go board that were inlaid with gold glitter.

云子

　　云子是特产于云南的围棋子，始创于唐代，在明清时期盛行全国，一直以来受到专业棋手和爱好者的推崇。云子的质地属于琉璃的一种，据史籍记载，其系以玛瑙石、紫瑛石合研为粉，再加上红丹粉（氧化铅）、硼砂等多种原料配合一起熔炼，然后用"长铁蘸其汁，滴以成棋"。最后，滴成的毛坯还要经过琢磨，才能成为大小一致的棋子。云子的制造工艺要求非常精细，其配方、火候、点子的手艺都是影响质量的重要因素。优质的云子造型统一规则，质地坚硬，表面平滑细腻，色泽柔美而不刺眼；在光亮下，黑子中心不透，周边有一种碧绿色光彩；白子温润如玉，呈现出淡淡的绿色。

- 云子
Yunzi

Yunzi

Yunzi is a type of Go stones manufactured in Yunnan Province of China, which first produced in the Tang Dynasty (618-907), then became popular in the Ming and Qing dynasties. It was the favorite stones of most professional and amateur players. It's a type of colored glaze. Based on historic records, it is sintered with the powder of agate, purple crystal and other mineral compounds like lead tetroxide and borax, and then "a long iron stick would dip in the compounds and created drops as Go stones". Finally, the semi-finished stones would be polished to become stones with identical size. The manufactory of Yunzi requires fine techniques, and carefully prepared formula, proper process, and superior workmanship. Good Yunzi have hard texture, consistent shape, smooth surface, and gentle hue. Under the light, the black Yunzi stones look opaque in the center and have translucent green hue, while the white Yunzi stones look similar to jade and have dim green light.

- 云子
  Yunzi

基本下法

1. 对局双方各执一色棋子，黑先白后，交替下子，每次只能下一子。

2. 棋子下在棋盘的交叉点上。

3. 棋子下定后，不得向其他点移动。

4. 轮流下子是双方的权利，但允许任何一方放弃下子权。

Basic Rules

I. One player plays the black stones, the other the while ones. They take turns to place one of their stones on a vacant point at each turn;

II. The stones are played on the intersections of the board;

III. Once a stone have been played, it cannot be moved to any other intersection;

IV. Players can take turns to place the stone, but either player may pass;

- 正确的执子手法

围棋执子的手法一般是以右手中指指肚与食指指背夹住棋子，行棋时以中指推着棋子轻轻一滑，棋子自然就会准确地落到点上，不仅避免棋子间相互碰撞，而且姿态自然、优雅，体现出下棋者的气质与修养，更体现了对棋局和对手的尊重。

Standard Way to Grip Go Stones

The standard way to hold a Go stone is gripping it between the index and middle fingers, with the middle finger on top, and then places it gently and directly on the desired intersection. In this way, it can avoid the clashes between stones. It also shows natural and elegant disposition and accomplishment of the player and pays respect to the game and the opponent.

棋子的气

一个棋子在棋盘上，与它直线紧邻的空点是这个棋子的"气"。棋子直线紧邻的点上，如果有同色棋子存在，那么它们便相互连接成一个不可分割的整体，它们的气也一并计算。棋子直线紧邻的点上如果有异色棋子存在，这口气就不复存在。如所有的气均为对方所占据，便呈无气状态，

Liberties of the Stone

"A liberty" is an open intersection next to a stone. If a stone is placed vertically or horizontally adjacent to another stone of the same color, the stones are connected and form an integrated unit with shared liberties. When a stone is placed vertically or horizontally adjacent to another stone of the opposite color, it takes a liberty away from the other stone. When all the liberties of a stone or a unit

这样的棋子不能在棋盘上存在，需要将其提出盘外，称为"提子"。

禁着点

如果一方在棋盘上某个交叉点落子后，这块棋子将呈现无气状态，而且也不能提走对方的子，棋盘上这个要落子的交叉点就称为该方的"禁着点"。围棋规则规定，不能在禁着点落子。

胜负的计算

围棋盘上共有361个交叉点，计算一盘棋的胜负就是由对局双方所占据交叉点的多少所决定的。更确切地说，就是由双方活棋所占据地域的大小来决定的。双方在经营和巩固自己的领地的同时，还要抵御对方棋子的入侵。而进攻和防守的基本方法就是设法包围对方的棋子，使其变为"死棋"。双方围绕着生与死进行一招一式的对抗与厮杀。棋盘上的区域完全划分完毕后，棋局即告终了。这时，双方需要通过计算，哪一方占的地域较多即为胜方。每方以180½子为归本数，超过此数者为胜，不足此数者为负。

of stones have been taken by the opposite side, the liberties are lost, and the stones cannot remain on the board, known as "removal of stones".

Forbidden Points

A forbidden point is an intersection on the board which, if occupied by a player's stone, would leave that stone without liberties, while failing to remove any opposing stones. A player cannot play on a forbidden point.

Calculation Method

As there are 361 intersections on the board, the results of the game depend on the number of enclosed intersections. In other words, the victory side has larger area of intersections with live stones. When the players enclose new empty points, they shall also defend their occupied area. Basically, attack and defense mean the players should try to enclose the opponent's stones. The two sides fight for life and death of the stones. Once the players can see no more useful moves and the game is over. At this time, the two sides need to compare whether they have larger total number of living stones and enclosed vacant points than the basic number 180½. The side that has larger score than 180½ will win and the side with lower score will lose.

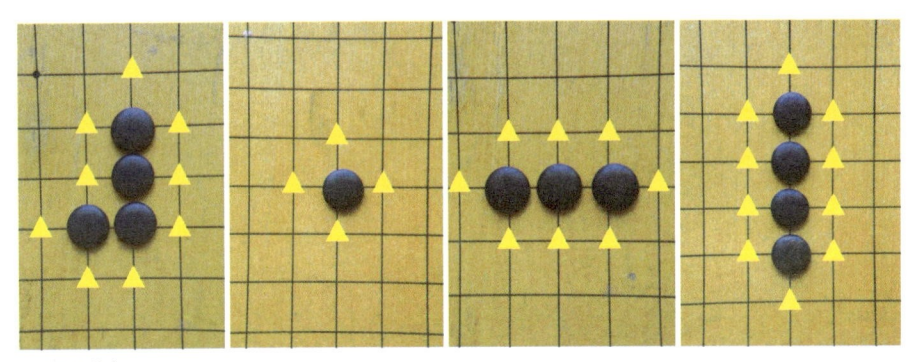

- 棋子的气

  图中标△处均为黑棋的"气"。

  Liberties of the Stones

  The points of △ in the diagram are liberties of black stones.

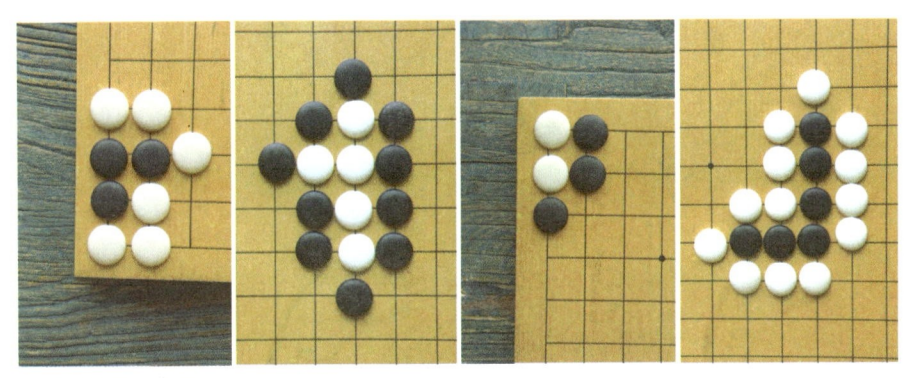

- 需要提子的情况

  Diagram of Captured Stones

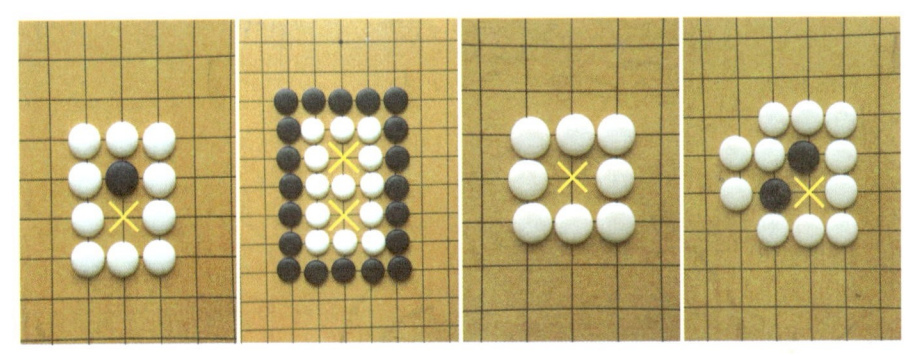

- 禁着点

  图中标×的地方都是黑棋的禁着点。

  Forbidden Points

  The points of × are forbidden points of black stones.

> 围棋与中国文化

围棋古代被列为"琴棋书画"文人四艺之一，与数学、兵法、诗歌、书画等中国传统文化的各个门类都有着千丝万缕的联系。

围棋与数学

围棋不仅是一种游戏，其圆形的棋子、方形的棋盘更契合了中国传统"天圆地方"的宇宙观，而棋子的黑白两色代表了昼夜阴阳的变化，棋盘上纵横的棋道构成了361个交叉点，除去中间的天元之外，恰好又是传统农历一年的天数。凡此种种，都为围棋蒙上了一层神秘色彩。甚至有人认为，围棋原是古代用于观测天象、占卜吉凶的工具。

围棋虽然只有黑子与白子，纵

> Go and Chinese Culture

Together with Chinese Guqin, calligraphy, and painting, Go has been known as one of the Four Accomplishments that must be mastered by Chinese literati in ancient time. Go has been closely connected with other subjects in traditional Chinese culture like mathematics, military tactics, poetry, calligraphy, and painting.

Go and Mathematics

Go is not just a game. The combination of round stones and the square board fits with ancient Chinese's view of the universe that "the sky is round and the land is square". The black and white colors represent the alternation of day and night. If excluding the central point, the 361 intersections on the board represent the number of days in Chinese lunar calendar. All these coincidences make Go

横十九路，其形式似乎简化到了极致，可是其中包含的变化却没有穷尽。宋代大科学家沈括在他写的科学技术著作《梦溪笔谈》中，曾推算过围棋到底有多少种变化。他的出发点是棋盘上每一个点有空子、黑子、白子3种可能，那么变化的总数就是3的361次方。这个数字究竟有多大呢？据数学家计算，$3^{361} > 1.74×10^{172}$。如果全世界50亿人都来下围棋，每人每天下一盘，要下完$1.74×10^{172}$这么多盘棋得花上至少

mysterious. It is said that Go was used as a tool for astrology and fortunetelling in ancient times.

Go has black and white stones and a board with 19 by 19 grids. It seems that it has the simplest form; however, it contains endless possible combinations. An ancient scientist named Shen Kuo in the Song Dynasty calculated the number of combinations of Go in his works named *Dream Pool Essays*. He supposed that each intersection on the board owns three possible situations, a white stone, a black stone, and being empty, and then the total number of potential combinations is 3 raised to 3's 361st power. How big is the number? According to mathematicians, $3^{361} > 1.74×10^{172}$, if all five billion people in the world come to play the Go every day, it takes $9.53×10^{159}$ years for them to complete the situations. Nevertheless, the history of universe is about 20 billion ($2×10^{10}$) years. Even if by adding together all the games played by people in the ancient and modern times since

* 沈括雕像（图片提供：微图）
Statue of Shen Kuo

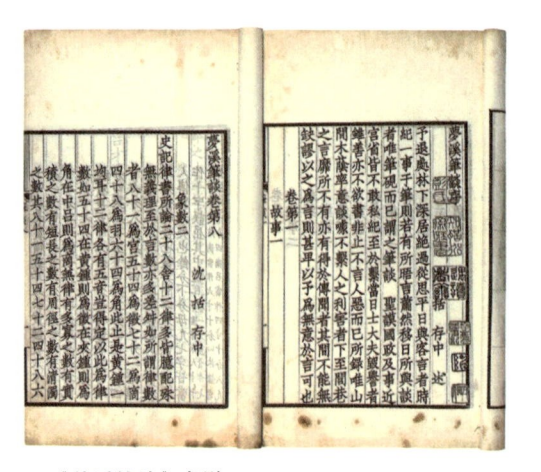

●《梦溪笔谈》书影
Photo Image of *Dream Pool Essays*

9.53×10^{159}年。而人类现在所知的宇宙的历史也不过200亿（2×10^{10}）年。自19道棋盘出现以来，即使把古今中外所有人下过的棋局加在一起，也只达到这个数字的极小一部分。因此，出现完全相同的棋局的概率几乎为零，围棋的变化也被人们形容为无穷无尽、神妙莫测。

围棋与军事

围棋是以双方在棋盘上所占区域的大小来判定胜负的棋类，对弈形式和两军作战十分相似。方正的棋盘代表着四海土地，黑白双方代表着双方的军队，而棋手则是各自

the 19 by 19 grids Go board appeared, the number of games is only a fraction. Therefore, the probability of having two exact same games is almost zero. Each game is unique and the possible combinations of Go is endless.

Go and Military Affairs

Go is an adversarial game and the winner is determined by the area of occupied territory on board, which is similar to the real battle. The square board represents land, the black and white stones represent the armies of two sides, and the two players are the commands of each side. As the victory of the Go is determined by the size territory, it is similar to the aim of war in ancient times. As the idiom goes, "Corner is gold, edge is silver, and center is grass." It means the four corners of the board are easy to keep, and then is the four edges, but the most difficult is to keep the center as an eye. Therefore, players of Go will firstly try to occupy the corner, and then the edge, finally the center. Similarly, many warlords in history also built their foundation in one section of China, and gradually

• 北京紫竹院公园的"跨海征东"棋局雕塑
Sculpture of the Scene "Crossing the Sea to Attack the East" in Purple Bamboo Park, Beijing

军队的指挥官。围棋的胜负是根据占地的多少来判定，这和古代大多数军事作战目的相同。围棋谚语有云："金角银边草肚皮。"是说棋盘的四角最容易做活，四边次之，而中腹最难做成活眼，所以下围棋时一般都先占角，再占边，逐渐占据中腹。而历史上许多开创霸业的军事家，也大都是先盘踞一方，逐渐发展壮大，待时机成熟，再逐鹿中原，统一天下。军队作战，士兵

grew more powerful. When they got the right opportunity, they would invade the central plain and try to take the whole country. During the fights, the mindset of the armies and commanders are important. During the fight in a board, when the two sides have matched levels, the judgments and mental attitudes are important. As an idiom of Go says: "one wrong step may cause the lost of the game."

In ancient times, many prominent

们的士气和指挥官的心态很重要，而在围棋的棋局上，双方水平差异不大时，对弈者的思路和心态尤为重要，正如棋谚所云："一着不慎，满盘皆输。"

历史上许多著名的军事家都爱好围棋，经常通过围棋的棋理研究用兵之法。而围棋理论家和一些著名棋手也常常借用兵法、战例来解释围棋，研究棋理。比如西汉时

militarists enjoyed playing Go, and often used the theories of Go to as a way to understand military strategies. Similarly, many famous Go theorists and players also learned from military strategies and cases of famous battles to explain and construct the theories of Go. In the Western Han Dynasty (206 B.C.-25 A.D.), Go was used as a way to learn military strategies. According to *Treatise on Classics from the Book*

• 古代战场上的进攻与防守
Attack and Defense on the Battlefield of Ancient Times

期，有人把围棋当作"兵法"；隋代史书《隋书·经籍志》也把围棋谱列入兵书一类。东汉哲学家桓谭在《新论》中甚至直截了当地说："俗有围棋，或言兵法之类也。"在桓氏以后几十年，著名经学家马融写过一篇著名的《围棋赋》，其中吟道："略观围棋兮，法于用兵。三尺之局兮，为战斗场。"他在文中论述道，下围棋要先占据要点，相当于棋盘上的星位，还要先保一角作为己方根据地，然后边地发展，扩张地盘，同时要注意自己势力的呼应和联络。

东汉末年的文学家应玚写过一篇《弈势》，就是从军事的角度来论述围棋理论的。文中以一些历史上有名的战例来说明围棋的战略战术。比如，书中举燕昭王和齐顷公在遭到失败后发奋图强的例子，说明围棋对局中如有局部的失误，就要加强自己，然后伺机进攻，以取得全局胜利。秦末楚汉相争中西楚霸王项羽失败的例子，说明围棋对局中切忌见利忘害、犹豫不决、当断不断、贪小失大等。

围棋能够修身养性、陶冶情

of *Sui*, Go tutorials were included in works of military strategies. Huan Tan, a philosopher lived in the Eastern Han Dynasty (25-220) commented in *Xinlun* (*New Theory*): "Go is a type of military strategies". Later, after Huan Tan passed away for a few decades, a famous Confucian scholar Ma Rong wrote a book named *Fu Poem of Go*, he said: "According to me, playing Go uses the same strategies as in a war, but the battlefield is on a much smaller board." He also mentioned that it is necessary to occupy vital positions first, such as the star points on the board, and occupy one corner as the foundation then gradually encroaching neighboring areas. Besides, communication between different sections was also important.

At the end of the Eastern Han Dynasty, Ying Yang wrote a paper named *Power of Go* to discuss theories of Go via the perspective of military strategies. In this paper, he used famous battles in history as examples to illustrate how these tactics would work in playing Go. For example, it mentioned that after the King Zhao of the State of Yan was defeated in the battle against the King Qing of the State Qi, he focused on making the nation stronger before initiating any subsequent

操。深谙棋术的军事指挥者则往往是个优秀的军事家。三国时期，曹魏政权的缔造者曹操、东吴的著名将领陆逊都酷爱围棋。东晋时的名相谢安也是一位喜爱围棋的军事家。晋太元八年（383），北方前秦政权的皇帝苻坚率百万大军南下，

attack. Similarly, after being defeated, it is important to strengthen the power before attacking the opponent's territory at the right moment in order to win the game. He also used the failure of Xiang Yu in the war between the State of Chu and the State of Han at the end of the Qin Dynasty (221 B.C.-206 B.C.) to refer to the importance of discarding greediness and hesitation.

Go can cultivate the players' moral characters and nourish their nature. Many excellent military commanders were also good at playing Go. During the Three Kingdoms Period (220-280), Cao Cao the founder of the regime of the Kingdom of Wei, and Lu Xun a commander of the State of Wu liked playing Go. Xie An, the famous prime minister and military commander of the Eastern Jin Dynasty was also found of Go. In the Eighth year of the reign of Emperor Taiyuan (383 A.D.), the Emperor Fu Jian of the State of the Early Qin in the north led a million soldiers to come to the south to try to

- 《东山报捷图》苏六朋（清）
Good News from the Eastern Mountain, by Su Liupeng (Qing Dynasty, 1616-1911)

准备一举消灭东晋。当时东晋的兵力十分薄弱，接到秦军兵抵淝水的消息后举国震动。晋帝在谢安的建议下，任命谢安的弟弟谢石为征讨大都督、谢安的侄子谢玄为先锋，率领8万晋军迎击敌军。谢石率军直抵淝水（今安徽寿县）东岸，与前秦军交战。结果东晋军队大获全胜。捷报传来的时候，谢安还在和宾客下围棋，接到快马送来的战报，看了一眼就顺手放在一边，不动声色，继续下棋。客人忍不住问他战事结果，他才轻描淡写地说："前方打了胜仗。"这段典故充分表现了谢安指挥若定的军事家风范。

围棋与诗歌

围棋有独特的游戏魅力，可以陶冶性情，有"坐隐""忘忧"之称。自东汉班固作《弈旨》以来，历朝历代涌现出了大量吟咏围棋的诗词歌赋。

唐朝是围棋兴盛的时代，又是诗歌的黄金时代，不仅涌现出许多围棋高手，而且不少著名的诗人都雅好围棋，写下了大量以棋为题材

conquer the Eastern Jin. At that time, Eastern Jin's military power was not strong. The whole nation was shocked when they knew the enemy army arrived at Feishui of Hebei Province. Under the suggestion of Xie An, Xie Shi, Xie An's younger brother was appointed as the chief commander, and Xie Xuan, Xie An's nephew as chief pioneer to lead eighty thousand soldiers to fight against Fu Jian. Xie Shi first came to the east side of Feishui (now Shouxian County in Anhui Province) and won the battle with the enemy army. When the good news came, Xie An was playing Go with a guest and he skimmed the report, and continued the game without showing any expression. When the guest could not help and asked him about the results of the battle, Xie An said: "We won." This story showed how calm Xie An was as a military commander.

Go and Poetry

Go not only has the unique charm as a game, it can also refine one's temperament, and is knows as "sitting in seclusion" and "forgetting worries". Since Ban Gu of the Eastern Han Dynasty (25-220) wrote the *Essence of Go,* many

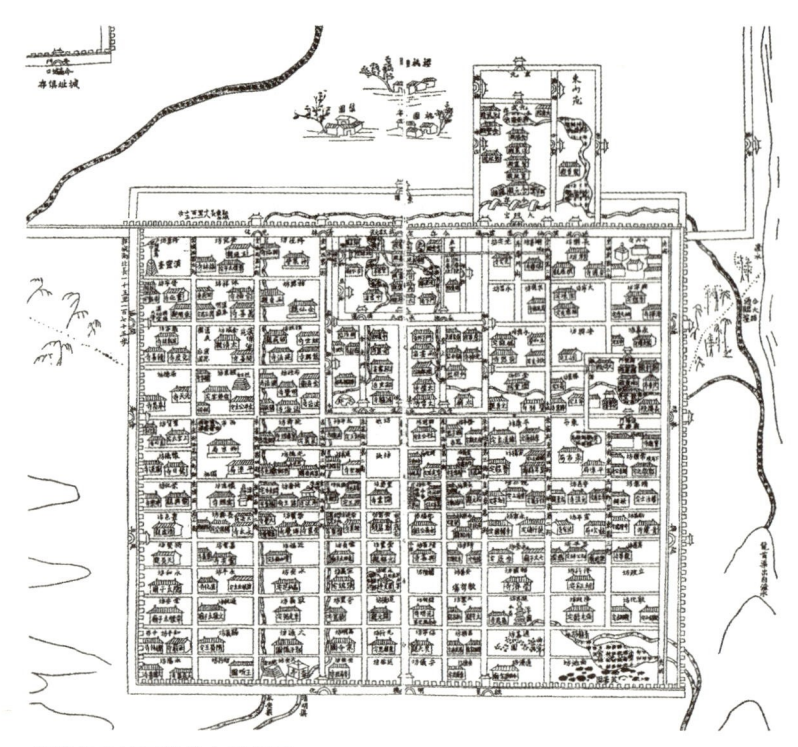

• 唐代长安城区域分布示意图
Sketch Map of Districts in Chang'an City (Tang Dynasty, 618-907)

的诗篇。

被誉为"诗圣"的大诗人杜甫就十分喜好围棋，常与几个朋友在一起酣战，忘记了时间的流逝。在杜甫脍炙人口的《秋兴八首》中，有这样两句诗："闻道长安似弈棋，百年世事不胜悲。"（听说长安时局多变，政坛的变化就像下棋一样，彼争此夺，反复不定，想到自己和大唐的命运，心中有说不尽

poems, verses, and rimes have been written for Go.

In the Tang Dynasty (618-907), Go was extremely popular, so as poetry. There were many good players of Go. Besides, there were many famous poets who were also fond of playing Go and wrote many poems about it.

Du Fu, the "Sage of Poetry" loved playing Go. He often played Go with friends and forgot the passage of time.

● 四川成都杜甫草堂
Thatched Cottage in Chengdu, Sichuan Province

的悲哀。）表达了安史之乱中杜甫忧国忧民的心绪。安史之乱后，杜甫回到长安，自称"且将棋度日，应用酒为年"。这种以棋、酒为伴的生活虽然看似散淡悠然，实际上表达了诗人寂寥的心境。杜甫的妻子出身名门，也喜好围棋，杜甫曾作诗道："老妻画纸为棋局，稚子敲针作钓钩。"记述了他与妻子画纸为棋盘，对弈娱乐的家庭趣事。杜

In his poem *Eight Poems of Autumn Feelings*, there are two verses: "I heard that the situation of Chang'an was volatile, the situation was as unpredictable as playing Go. When I think about my own fate and our country, I have endless grief in my mind." The verses expressed Du Fu's concern for the country. After the Anshi Rebellion, Du Fu returned to Chang'an and told others that "I live by playing Go and drinking alcohol." This kind of lifestyle seemed to be enjoyable, but it revealed his helplessness. Du Fu's wife was born in a rich family and also liked playing Go. Du Fu once wrote: "my wife drew Go board on paper and my kids knocked pins as hooks", which described interesting family leisure time that his wife drew the lines on paper for playing Go with him. Among all his poems about Go, the two verses in *Two Poems Written on the Water Pavilion of Zhongming Prefecture on July 1st* are the most attractive. These two verses are said as follows: "It is cloudy and rainy in the Chujiang River and Wuxia Valley; I stand by the waterfall and watch my friends playing Go", which are regarded as an aesthetic description of playing Go and creates a pure and profound atmosphere.

甫留下的众多咏棋诗歌中，以《七月一日题终明府水楼二首》中的两句写得最美："楚江巫峡半云雨，清簟疏帘看弈棋。"诗句描摹入微，境界清远，意趣幽深，被视为观棋的画境。

唐代中期的大诗人元稹和白居易并称"元白"。他们二人友情深厚，不仅以诗齐名，而且都酷好围棋。长庆元年（821），元稹邀请朋友到府中举行棋会，并写下了《酬段丞与诸棋流会宿弊居见赠二十四韵》，是吟咏围棋的长诗之一。作

• 元稹像
Portrait of Yuan Zhen

Yuan Zhen and Bai Juyi, the two poets lived in the middle of the Tang Dynasty, were known as "Yuan-Bai". They were good friends, and were not only famous for poems, but also loved playing Go. In the first year of Emperor Changqing (821 A.D.), Yuan Zhen invited his friends to come play Go together at his place and wrote *24-line for Duan Cheng and Go Players in My Home*, which is the longest poem in history under the theme of Go. In this poem, the author described the fierce fights on the Go board and the happy mood of these Go players. When someone asked why he liked playing Go, and he answered in his poem: "Playing Go is extremely fun, which is not known by mediocrities."

Bai Juyi was not only fond of Go, but also good at playing Go. He once wrote: "If I am happy, I will drink some wine; if I am bored, I will play Go." In this famous poem *By the Pond*, he wrote: "Two monks sit opposite to each other and play Go in the mountain. The bamboo shadow on the board is dark and clear. There is no other sound but the clicks of the stones." With only a few words, he depicted the scene that there was a bamboo forest covered by warm

• 《香山九老图》吴嘉猷（清）

白居易晚年长居河南洛阳城南的香山寺，时常邀请胡杲、吉旼、郑据、刘真、卢贞、张浑、李元爽和禅僧如满这八位老人在香山聚会，开怀畅饮，吟诗对弈，极尽欢娱，号为"香山九老"。

Nine Old Man of the Xiangshan Mountain, by Wu Jiayou (Qing Dynasty, 1616-1911)

In Bai Juyi's last years, he lived in the Xiangshan Temple that was situated at the south of Luoyang City of Henan Province. He often invited other eight friends, including Hu Gao, Ji Min, Zheng Ju, Liu Zhen, Lu Zhen, Zhang Hun, Li Yuanshuang, and the Monk Ru Man to get together in Xiangshan Temple to drink and to write poems. They were known as Nine Old Men Of the Xiangshan Mountian.

者在诗中描绘了这次棋会上各方搏杀斗智的热烈场面，及爱棋人乐而忘忧的心情。有人问元稹围棋到底有什么乐趣，元稹在诗中答道："此中无限兴，唯怕俗人知。"（围棋的无穷乐趣是凡夫俗子无法知道的。）

白居易不仅嗜好下棋，而且棋艺颇高。诗云："兴发饮数杯，闷

sunshine. There was no other sound except for the sound of playing Go. The verses create a peaceful atmosphere and a detached sentiment from possessions.

In Du Xunhe's poem *Watching Go Game*, there are verses: "They are sitting opposite to each other and using stones as soldiers. Sometimes, they attack the opponent, sometimes they focus on defense. To win the battle, they have to enlarge the enclosed territory and to capture opposite stones at the right moment. When they meet rivals, they cannot finish the game until midnight." With concise and vivid language, the poet depicted the scenario that the two players attempted to protect their own territory and attempted to win the game.

来棋一局。"白居易吟咏围棋的著名诗作《池上二绝》其一写道："山僧对棋坐，局上竹阴清。映竹无人见，时闻下子声。"寥寥数笔，再现了两个僧人在一片竹林中对坐下棋的场景：和煦的阳光映照着这片竹林，但却看不见人的影子，只有对弈落子的声音阵阵传来。整首诗意境幽静闲雅，高远淡泊。

晚唐诗人杜荀鹤的《观棋》

They would capture the opposite stones if the opponent faced other crises and they would occupy more territory if they had taken the upper side. This poem shows the obsession of the players with Go.

In the early Song Dynasty, most literati liked playing Go and paid great attention to improve their skills. Fan Zhongyan, a famous Prime Minister in the Northern Song Dynasty was also a great literati and poet. Aside from political affairs, he often commented on Go. For example, he once wrote : "I just want to be drunk when I urged the guests to drink and I will spare my opponent when I take the upper hand."

Great literati Su Shi liked playing Go as well, but he did not reach a high

《十八学士图》局部 佚名（宋）
唐高祖年间，秦王李世民（唐太宗）在宫城以西开文学馆，罗致各方文士，共有杜如晦、房玄龄、陆德明等十八人。这些人在一起研究文献，商略古今，作诗下棋，号为"十八学士"。后来"十八学士"成为后世画家青睐的题材之一。

Chinese Painting: *Eighteen Literati*, by Anonymity (Part) (Song Dynasty, 960-1279)

During the reign of Emperor Gaozu of Tang Dynasty (618-907), Prince Qin (Emperor Taizong) Li Shimin opened an academy at the west side of the palace and recruited scholars from all over the country. The leading eighteen ones included Du Ruhui, Fang Xuanling, and Lu Deming, etc. They worked together to study historic records, discuss past events and current affairs, write poems, and play Go. They were known as the Eighteen Scholars and became one of the favorite themes of subsequent painters.

诗云："对面不相见，用心同用兵。算人常欲杀，顾己自贪生。得势侵吞远，乘危打劫赢。有时逢敌手，当局到深更。"诗人用简练而生动的语言，写出了对战双方总想保全自己，置对方于死地，时时乘危打劫，得势时想抢占更大地盘的心理状态，表现出下棋者对围棋的痴迷。

宋初的文人士大夫都喜好围棋，而且比较注重对棋艺的研究。

- 杭州苏东坡纪念馆的苏东坡像

Statue of Su Dongpo (Su Shi) in the Su Dongpo's Museum of Hangzhou City, Zhejiang Province

level, and thus did not frequently play the game. Nevertheless, he enjoyed watching others play Go and he grasped the essence of Go. He did not care about if he lost or won. He once wrote a famous poem, named *Watching Go Game* and mentioned that the fun of playing Go was about entertainment and relaxation. Thus, he said: "Victory is a happy thing, so as defeat". These two verses showed his feelings towards his own bitter and sweet moments in life. His attitude towards Go had great influence on subsequent literati and the development of Go.

Poet Zhao Shixiu of the Song Dynasty (960-1279) once wrote *Waiting for a Friend.* He wrote: "During the raining season, it rains everywhere. I hear the sounds of frogs from the pound with green grasses. It is now after the midnight, but my guest has not been here, so I tap on the Go board with stones, which shatters the snuff." This poem depicts the scenario that the poet was waiting for his guest in a rainy mid night and expressed his disappointed mood by creating a quiet and relaxed atmosphere with the action of "knocking the Go stones". This poem sounds natural and fresh, just like how life is.

范仲淹是北宋一代名相，又是诗文大家。他为政之余常寄情棋枰，曾写道："恶劝酒时图共醉，痛赢棋处肯相饶。"

诗词书画无一不通的大文豪苏轼虽然也好围棋，棋艺却不甚精湛，因此不常下棋。但他喜欢观棋，在旁观者的角度悟出许多棋机棋理，对于输赢却毫不在意。他曾写下著名的《观棋》一诗，认为围

Go and Painting

As Go has been regarded as one of the refined pursuits, it appeared in paintings in early era.

Gu Kaizhi, a famous painter of the Eastern Jin Dynasty had a painting named *Playing Go in the Water Pavilion*. The Water Pavilion is surrounded by water. It has three stories and windows on each direction, thus has a good view. It is a perfect place to invite friends over for tea and playing Go.

In 1972, a fraction of folding screen painting named the *Fair Lady Who Plays Go* was unearthed from a tomb of the Tang Dynasty in Turpan of Xinjiang

● 《西园雅集图》华嵒（清）

"西园"指的是北宋英宗时的驸马都尉王诜的宅院。当时的著名文人如苏轼、米芾、黄庭坚等曾在此聚会，博弈、作诗、绘画、弹琴。《西园雅集图》成为宋元以来人物画家描绘文人集会的传统题材。

Elegant Gathering in the West Garden, by Hua Yan (Qing Dynasty, 1616-1911)

"Western Garden" refers to the house of the Emperor Yingzong's son-in-law, Wang Shen of the Northern Song Dynasty (960-1127). Famous literati, Su Shi, Mi Fu, and Huang Tingjian often got together there to play game, write poem, paint, and play Chinese Guqin. *Elegant Gathering in the West Garden* had been a traditional theme to describe social gathering of literati since the Song and Yuan dynasties.

棋的乐趣在于娱乐、陶情，因此"胜固欣然，败亦可喜"。这两句诗实际上是他一生起落坎坷，几经波折之后的感慨。他对围棋的态度对后世文人以及围棋的发展产生了深远的影响。

宋代诗人赵师秀的《约客》，也是一首脍炙人口的咏棋名作。"黄梅时节家家雨，青草池塘处处蛙。有约不来过夜半，闲敲棋子落灯花。"诗中大意是：梅子黄时，处处都在下雨，长满青草的池塘边上，传来阵阵蛙声。时已过午夜，已约请好的客人还没有来，我无聊地用棋子在棋盘上轻轻敲击，震落了灯花。全诗通过对撩人思绪的环境的描写及对"闲敲棋子"这一细节动作的渲染，既写出了诗人雨夜候客来访的情景，也写出一种怅惘失落的心情，意境清新自然，充满了生活气息。

围棋与绘画

围棋自古以来被看作是一种风雅的活动，很早就出现在各类绘画作品中。

Uygur Autonomous Region. This painting is centered at the lady who plays Go and also depicts the observers, attendants, and playful children. With a high hair buns, the lady is holding a Go stone with a life-like pondering expression. The plump body, luxurious clothes reveal that people in the Tang Dynasty preferred plump and gaudy women.

Playing Go under the Double Screen painted by Zhou Wenju of the Five dynasties and Ten states is a famous work depicting the scene of playing Go. In the painting, it shows Li Jing, the second Emperor of the Later Tang Dynasty is playing Go with his brothers, Jingsui, Jingda, and Jingti. Li Jing who wears a tall hat and holds a tray salver is sitting in the middle and watching the game. The two players are Jingda and Jingti. The appearances ad expressions of the figures were carefully painted with refined skills. The lines depicting their clothes were thin, winding, and powerful. With the realistic depiction of the furniture, it reflects a real life situation.

In the Northern Song and Southern Song dynasties, with the increasing popularity of Go among scholars, more

东晋时期的大画家顾恺之曾作《水阁会棋图》。水阁是四面临水的楼阁，阁高三层，四面敞窗，远眺江山如画，在这个地方邀请三二知己品茗弈棋，真是人生最惬意的事。

1972年在新疆吐鲁番的一座唐墓中出土了屏风画《弈棋仕女图》的残片。画面以弈棋的贵妇为中心，又有亲近观棋、侍婢应候、儿童嬉戏等内容。画中的下棋的贵妇发束高髻，举棋沉思，神情描绘得惟妙惟肖。贵妇丰满的肌体，华丽的服饰，反映出盛唐时期以丰腴、浓艳为美的风尚。

五代时期的画家周文矩所画《重屏会棋图》也是著名的棋画。图中描绘的是南唐中主李璟与弟弟景遂、景达、景逖会

works about Go were accomplished. Famous painters, including Shi Ke, Sun Zhiwei, Liu Songnian, Li Tang, Ma Yuan, and Xia Gui all had paintings about Go.

There are many paintings about Go from the Ming Dynasty (1368-1644). At that time, a lot of famous artists were enthusiastic about Go, and they often used Go as the theme of their painting. For example, painters, like Shen Zhou, Zhou Chen, Qiu Ying, Xu Wei all painted about playing Go,

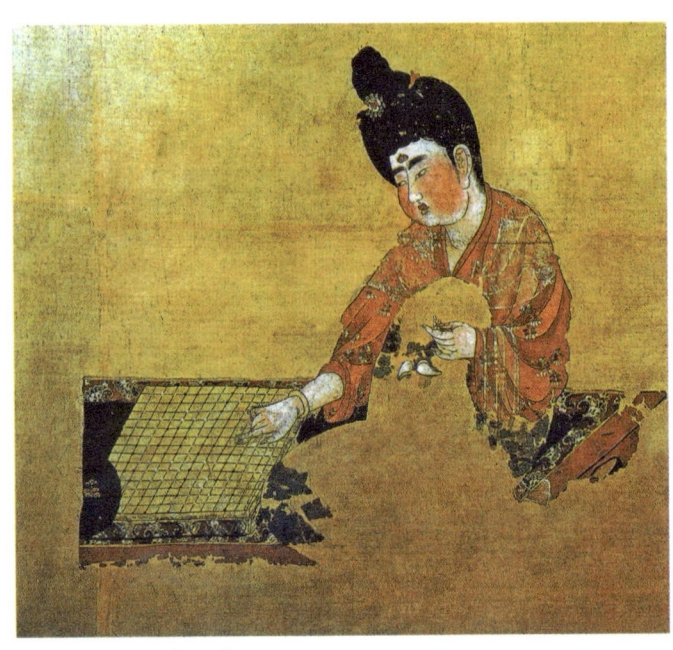

- 《弈棋仕女图》（唐）
Fair Lady Who Plays Go (Tang Dynasty, 618-907)

《重屏会棋图》周文矩（五代）

图中背景是一架大屏风，屏风绘有醉酒图，画中又有一架小屏，屏中有屏，故名"重屏"。

Playing Go under the Double Screen, by Zhou Wenju (Five Dynasties and Ten States, 907-960)

The background of the painting is a big screen. On the screen, it has the scene of getting drunk and a smaller screen. As the smaller screen is painted on the bigger screen, there are two screens together, known as the "double screen".

棋的情景。李璟头戴高帽，手持盘盒，居中观棋，而对弈者是景达和景遂。人物容貌和表情刻画精细，衣纹细劲曲折，再加上周围的陈设十分写实，体现出一种浓郁的生活气息。

两宋时期，随着围棋进一步受到文人的青睐，以围棋入画的文人画也层出不穷。著名的画家石恪、孙知微、刘松年、李唐、马远、夏珪等人都留下过以弈棋

but their contents focused on different aspects. For example, Shen Zhou's *Watching Go* is about current era, while Zhou Chen's *Four Hermits Playing Go* centered on past events, but their themes were all related with scholar-bureaucrats' aesthetic pursuit and interests in playing Go and hiding away from the society. Qiu Ying, Tang Yin, Shen Zhou, and Wen Zhengming have been known as Four Great Painters of the Ming Dynasty. Qiu Ying and Tang

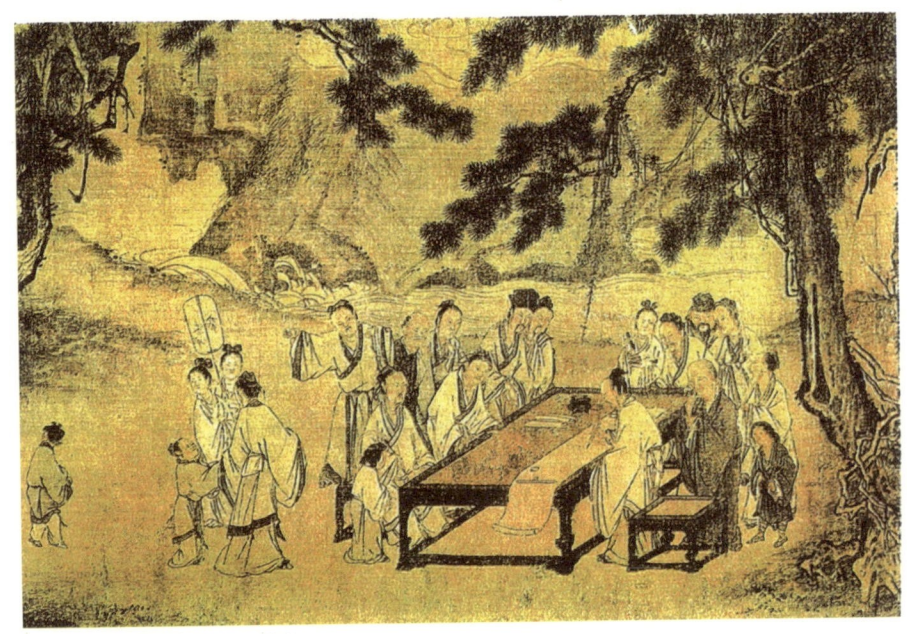

• **《西园雅集图》马远（宋）**
Elegant Gathering in the West Garden, by Ma Yuan (Song Dynasty, 960-1279)

为题材的画作。

明代留下的围棋画很多。许多著名画家自己就是围棋爱好者，因此常将围棋作为他们创作的素材，如沈周、周臣、仇英、徐渭等都有围棋画传世。从明代围棋画的内容看，有表现现实题材的，如沈周《观弈图》，也有表现历史题材的，如周臣《四皓弈棋图》，但主旨都在表现士大夫"手谈""坐隐"的雅兴和意趣。仇英、唐寅、

Yin were once Zhou Chen's apprentices and Wen Zhengming learned painting from Shen Zhou for a while. Therefore, the four had master-apprentice relation and friendship. As all of them liked Go, they also played Go aside from talking about painting.

Go and Novels

In the Ming and Qing dynasties, with the development of popular culture, novels were popular among all social classes.

- 《汉宫春晓图》中的弈棋情景 仇英（明）

  "汉宫春晓"是中国人物画的传统题材。这幅作品为长卷形式，描绘了宫女的群像，又融入琴棋书画、鉴古、莳花等休闲活动，是历史故事画中的精彩之作。

  A Scenario Depicting Playing Go in the Painting: *Spring Arrives at the Palace of Han Dynasty*, by Qiu Ying (Ming Dynasty, 1368-1644)

  Spring Arrives at the Palace of Han Dynasty is a traditional theme in Chinese portrait painting. On a long paper, it depicts the images of these beauties and illustrates their leisure activities including playing Chinese Guqin and Go, calligraphy, painting, appreciating antiques, and growing flowers, which is an excellent image painting in history.

- 《泼墨十二段之四》徐渭（明）

  徐渭，字文长，明代写意派的著名画家。他十分热爱围棋，留有多幅以围棋为题材的画作，也写有一些围棋诗。

  Twelve Parts in Splash-Ink No.4, by Xu Wei (Ming Dynasty, 1368-1644)

  Xu Wei, courtesy name Wenchang, was a famous impressionistic painter of the Ming Dynasty. He was found of playing Go and created many paintings and some poems about Go.

• 《溪亭对弈图》唐寅（明）
Playing Go in Pavilion, by Tang Yin (Ming Dynasty, 1368-1644)

Thus, Go, which had already been an important part of the leisure activities, was mentioned frequently in novels.

In the collection of short stories, named *Amazing Stories* (Vol.II) written by the novelist, Ling Mengchu, there was a story that the young taoist defeated all the masters in world and the female's life was affected by two games. In the story, the main female character opened an academy of Go, and recruited several students. This story reflects the popularity of Go at that time which is consistent with historic records.

One of China's four classical novels, *Romance of the Three Kingdoms*, mentioned that many powerful people were fond of playing Go and compared it with deploying soldiers and traps on the battlefield. There was a well-known situation about it. The general Guan Yu of the Kingdom of Shu-Han

沈周、文徵明合称"明四家"，其中仇英、唐寅曾师从周臣学画，文徵明也曾师从沈周学画。"明四家"半师半友，常聚在一起切磋围棋和绘画。

- **《三国演义》绣像**

  《三国演义》是中国第一部长篇章回体历史小说，主要表现了魏、蜀、吴三个统治集团相互间的斗争，在广阔的背景下，展现了一幕幕波澜起伏的战争场面。

  Tapestry: *Romance of the Three Kingdoms*

  The *Romance of the Three Kingdoms* was the first historic novel with each chapter headed by a couplet giving the gist of its content. This novel reflects the mutual struggle among the Kingdom of Wei, the Kingdom of Shu-Han, and the Kingdom of Wu. It also depicts many important battles with one climax following another in a grand background.

  ## 围棋与小说

  明清时期，随着市民文化的蓬勃发展，小说这种文学形式受到各阶层人士的欢迎。而已经成为人们休闲生活重要组成部分的围棋，也大量地出现在小说中。

  明代小说家凌濛初所著的短篇小说集《二刻拍案惊奇》里，就有"小道人一着饶天下，女棋童两局注终身"的故事。故事里的女主角自己开设了棋馆，招揽学生教授围棋。这反映出当时围棋的普及程度，和正史中对围棋繁荣的记载是一致的。

  中国四大古典名著之一的章回小说《三国演义》中，提到的许多三国时期叱咤风云的人物都爱好下

  was shot by an arrow in the battle at Fang Cheng. As the arrow head was poisonous, his right arm could not move. When the great doctor Hua Tuo arrived, he found the poison got to the bone and had to cut off the muscle and skin to scrape the poison off the bone. During the surgical operation, all the people around were frightened, but Guan Yu continued to drink alcohol and play Go, as if nothing had happened.

棋，并且将围棋与战场上的排兵布阵相类比。小说中有个至今脍炙人口的段落：蜀汉大将关羽在率军攻打樊城时，被射中一箭。由于箭头有毒，关羽右臂青肿不能活动。当时的神医华佗闻讯赶来，诊断发现箭毒已经入骨，于是决定割开皮肉，刮去骨头上的箭毒。手术进行中，周围的人心惊胆战，关羽却依然饮酒下棋，若无其事。

明代世情小说《金瓶梅》中深入描写了市民阶层的围棋活动，作者兰陵笑笑生本人就是个有相当水平的围棋高手，因此书中对围棋的对弈过程叙述得很到位。据统计，

In *Jinpingmei* (*Golden Lotus*), a novel written in the Ming Dynasty (1368-1644), it vividly described the situations of the ordinary people playing Go. The author Lanling Xiaoxiaosheng himself reached a considerable high level of Go, thus his description of the playing was quite accurate. It was found that there were tens of scenarios where playing Go was mentioned. From the description of the book, Go had become a favorite pastime and indispensable recreational activities of the people lived in the Ming Dynasty.

Wu Cheng'en, a scholar of the Ming Dynasty, enjoyed playing Go. In his novel *Journey to the West*, there are

• 日本画家所描绘的关公刮骨疗毒
Guan Yu Receiving the Treatment of Bone Scrapping, by Japanese Painter

《金瓶梅》一书中描写下棋的地方有十几处。从书中的描写可以看出，围棋已经成为明代市民阶层喜爱的消遣，是他们生活中很普通而又不可缺少的文娱活动。

明代文人吴承恩对围棋十分痴迷，所以他写的《西游记》中也少不了围棋的情节。第九回就描写了唐代名臣魏徵在梦斩泾河老龙之前，唐太宗召他下棋的情节。书中还引述了《烂柯经》（即《棋经十三篇》）中《合战篇》的全文。还有第二十六回，孙悟空在五庄观打坏了人参果树，为求救树的仙方，他来到蓬莱仙岛求助于福、禄、寿三星，看到他们正在下围棋。连仙人都爱好围棋，可见围棋在作者心目中的地位。

清代小说家曹雪芹所著的《红楼梦》里，描写和提到围棋的地方有16处。书中的主要角色贾宝玉、林黛玉、贾迎春、贾探春、贾惜春、妙玉、薛宝钗、薛宝琴、香菱、冯紫英等许多角色都下围棋。书中第八十回有这样一段描写：

只见妙玉低着头，问惜春道："你这个'畸角儿'不要了么？"

many situations about Go. In Chapter Nine, it described the famous court official Wei Zheng of the Tang Dynasty was summoned by the Emperor Taizong to play Go with him before he killed the Dragon King of Jinghe River in his dream. The book cited the whole text of a chapter named the *Battle* in the *Rotted Handle of the Axe* (also called *The Thirteen Stories of Go*). In Chapter Twenty-six, after the Monkey King destroyed the sapodilla plum tree in Wuzhuang Taoist Temple, he came to Penglai Fairy Island to visit the three immortals — Fu (Happiness), Lu (Fortune), Shou (Longevity) and saw they were playing Go. This shows how importance of Go in the heart of the author, for even the fairies like playing Go.

Dream of the Red Mansion written by Cao Xueqin, the novelist in the Qing Dynasty mentioned about playing Go for sixteen times. The main characters in the book, including Jia Baoyu, Lin Daiyu, Jia Yingchun, Jia Tanchun, Jia Xichun, Miaoyu, Xue Baochai, Xue Baoqin, Xiangling, and Feng Ziying, etc., who all know how to play Go. In Chapter Eighty, there is a scenario below:

Miaoyu, her head lowered, asked,

孙温绘《全本红楼梦》中的围棋场景
Scenario of Playing Go in the *Complete Compilation of the Dream of Red Mansion*, by Sun Wen

惜春道："怎么不要？你那里头都是死子儿，我怕什么。"妙玉却微微笑着，把边上子一接，却搭转一吃，把惜春的一个角儿都打起来了，笑着说道："这叫作'倒脱靴势'。"

这段写妙玉下棋举重若轻，棋艺高妙，"倒脱靴势"这个围棋术语使用自然，十分生动，可见作者曹雪芹也是一位围棋高手。

"Don't you want this corner?" "Of course I do." said Xichun, "Your pieces there are all dead. What am I afraid of ? " Miaoyu was smiling, linked her pieces into one continuous border and counterattacked, threatening Xichun's corner. "This is called *pulling off the boot backward*." she chuckled.

This shows that Miaoyu is good at playing Go. The term "pulling off the boot backward" was used properly under this situation, which revealed that the author Cao Xueqin must be a good Go player.

中国象棋
Chinese Chess

　　中国象棋是一种在中国流传十分广泛的棋类游戏。下棋双方根据自己对棋局形势的理解和对棋艺规律的掌握来调动车马，组织兵力，协调作战，在棋盘这块特定的战场上进行着象征性的军事战斗。

The Chinese chess prevails widely across China. The players deploy their pieces to perform a coordinated attack or defense based on their knowledge to the chess situation and rules. It is a symbolic battle presented on the chess board.

> 中国象棋的源流

中国象棋的渊源可以追溯到距今两千多年前的战国时期。"象棋"一词最早出现在《楚辞·招魂》中："菎蔽象棋，有六簙些。分曹并进，道相迫些。成枭而牟，呼五白些。"意思是说，用玉石做成的象棋子，每方共有六颗；比赛的方法是两人对局，相互进攻，逼迫对手；最后赢者击败了敌兵，发出了胜利的欢呼。不过这里说的象棋不是今天的中国象棋，而是当时一种十分流行的棋戏，叫作"六博"，可以说是象棋的雏形。由此可见，早期的象棋就是象征军事组织和战斗场面的一种游戏。英国著名学者李约瑟博士在其著作《中国科学文化史》中详尽分析了六博与天文、象术、数学的关系，他说：

> Origin of Chinese Chess

The origin of Chinese chess can trace back to the Warring States Period (475 B.C.-221 B.C.) more than 2,000 years ago. The term Chinese chess (*Xiangqi*) firstly appeared in the famous book *The Elegies of Chu* State (chapter: *Summons of the Soul*): "With jade chess pieces, each side holds 6 pieces; sides are taken; they advance together; keenly they threaten each other; finally one beats the other and hails for the victory." But the chess mentioned here is not today's Chinese chess, yet a very popular board game at that time called "Liubo" which is considered the origin of Chinese chess. Thus it can be seen that the early Chinese chess is a game representing military organization and battle field. Famous British scholar Dr. Joseph Needham once discussed the relationship between Liubo and astronomy, Taoist theory

"只有在中国，阴阳理论的盛行促使象棋雏形的产生，带有天文性质的占卜术得以发明，继而发展成带有军事含义的一种游戏。"

秦汉到三国时期，象棋的形制不断变化。南北朝时期，北周武帝（561—578在位）制《象经》，庾信写《象戏经赋》，标志着象棋形制改革的完成。

隋唐时期，象棋活动稳步开展，史籍上屡见记载。其中最重要的是唐代名相牛僧孺所著《玄怪录》中关于宝应元年（762）岑顺梦见象戏的一段故事。从这则故事可以知道，宝应年间的象戏就是今日象棋的前身，已有将、车、马、卒等兵种，而且步法与现在的象棋已

- 铜质象棋子（宋）
Copper Chinese Chess Pieces (Song Dynasty, 960-1279)

and mathematics in his book *Science and Civilization in China*, as quoted: "Only in China, the prevalence of Yin-Yang Theory can promote the birth of the origin form of Chinese chess. With ancient Divination relating to astronomy, it was later developed into a board game with strong military features."

From the Qin and Han dynasties to the Three Kingdoms Period, the form and rules of Chinese chess continuously changed. In the Southern and Northern dynasties, during the reign of Emperor Wu of Northern Zhou Dynasty (561-578), the government issued *The Classic of Chinese Chess*, along with the *Notes and Proses of Chinese Chess* written by Yu Xin, which marked the completion of the form and rules' reform of Chinese chess.

In the Sui and Tang dynasties, Chinese chess developed gradually and stably. Among its repetitious appearance in the historic records, the most important one is in the *Tales of the Obscure and Peculiar* written by Niu Sengru, a famous Prime Minister in the Tang Dynasty referring the story of Cen Shun's dreaming about *Xiangxi* happened in 762 A.D. According to this story, *Xiangxi* in the Period Baoying is the origin of modern Chinese chess which already

很接近。这种象戏又被称为"宝应象棋",至今日本还将它作为象棋的代称。

唐代以前,象棋只有将、车、马、卒四种棋。据《唐书》记载,当时出现了发射石子用于攻城的机械,称为"将军砲",所以象棋中的"砲"一直为"石"字旁。唐代武器的进步,促进了模仿战斗场面的象棋的发展,象棋又增加了砲、士、象三个兵种,和现代象棋基本相似了。当时象棋的流行情况,从诗文传奇的诸多记载中都可略见一斑。而早期的象棋谱《樗薄象戏格》三卷则可能是唐代的著作。

- 瓷质象棋子(南宋)
Porcelain Chinese Chess Pieces
(Southern Song Dynasty, 1127-1279)

included the pieces of lord, chariot, horse, and pawn and obeyed the rules similar to present Chinese chess game. It is also called "Baoying chess" which is still the alternative name for Chinese chess in Japan.

Before the Tang Dynasty, Chinese chess only had four kinds of pieces including lord, chariot, horse and pawn. According to the *Book of Tang Dynasty*, there appeared a military device used for launching stones to attack the castle, called the "General Cannon" (砲). So the piece of Chinese chess has been always carved with the character 砲 (*Pao*) with stone (石) as its radical instead of 炮 (*Pao*) with fire (火). The new breakthrough in military weapon in the Tang Dynasty contributed to the development of chess including the pieces of cannon, guard and elephant to the Chinese chess which imitated the situation in battle field. Then it is almost the same with the modern one. The prevalence of Chinese chess can be seen in many verses and articles at that time. And the first notation of Chinese chess *Chubo Chinese Chess's Notes* (with 3 volumes) might be completed in the Tang Dynasty.

In the Song Dynasty (960-1279), the

到了宋代，象棋广泛流行。北宋时期，先后有司马光的《七国象戏》、尹洙的《象戏格》和《棋势》、晁补之的《广象戏图》等象棋著作问世，民间还流行一种"大象戏"。晁补之的广象棋，棋子32个，与现代象棋的棋子总数相同，棋盘纵横各十一路，比现代象棋盘大一点。摆棋时将两砲放在车的外侧，而棋子名称和着法与现代象棋相同。

南宋高宗时，一位法号与咸的僧人在其相关著作中曾记载道："今以板画路，中间界之以河，各设十六子：卒、砲、车、马、象等，俗谓象棋者也。"由此看来，当时的象棋已与今天完全一样了。南宋时期，象棋成为流行极为广泛的棋艺活动。李清照、刘克庄、洪遵、文天祥等著名的文人和士大夫都嗜好下象棋。宫廷设的"棋待诏"中，象棋手占一半以上。民间有称为"棋师"的象棋业者和专制象棋子和象棋盘的手工业者。南宋还出现了洪迈的《棋经论》、叶茂卿的《象棋神机集》、陈元靓的《事林广记》等多种有关象棋著述。

Chinese chess still gained its momentum. In the Northern Song Dynasty, there were series of relevant books published including *Chinese Chess of Seven Kingdoms* by Sima Guang, *Notes of Chinese Chess* and *Questions about Chinese Chess*, by Yin Zhu, and the *Illustrated Notes of Guangxiangxi* by Chao Buzhi. And there appeared game called "*Daxiangxi*" among the folks. The game of *Guangxiangxi* invented by Chao Buzhi has 32 pieces, which is the same with the modern Chinese chess. With eleven grids both vertically and horizontally, its board is bigger than the modern Chinese chess and with two pieces of cannon on the two flanks of the two pieces of chariots. Then the name of the chess piece and rules are same with the modern one.

In the reign of Emperor Gaozong in the Southern Song Dynasty, a monk with the religious title of Yuxian once mentioned in his relevant books: "Today, people draw the grids on stone board and add a river as the boundary in the middle. The game includes 16 chess pieces namely pawn, cannon, chariot, horse, elephant and etc. This game is called *Xiangqi* (Chinese chess)" So clearly, the game at that time was exactly same with

宋太祖下棋

相传宋太祖赵匡胤喜爱象棋,棋艺高超,一生罕有败局,自以为天下无敌。赵匡胤当皇帝以前,曾在全国各地游览。一天他走到华山地界,听说山上有一位名叫陈抟的象棋高手,就走进山中和陈抟对弈。陈抟预知赵匡胤将做皇帝,就想和他开个玩笑。陈抟故意把自己的棋下成看似必败的局面(赵匡胤为黑方,陈抟为红方)。赵匡胤看到自己的棋形势大好,认为自己肯定会赢。陈抟说:"如我取胜,你将来得天下时就把华山输给我。"赵匡胤既不相信自己将来能当皇帝,更不相信自己会输棋,就一口答应下来。没想到几步之后自己众多棋子竟挡不住陈抟单马的进攻。赵匡胤输得目瞪口呆,对陈抟高超的棋艺佩服得五体投地。后来赵匡胤果真当上了皇帝,只好履行诺言,并永远免除华山周围地区赋税。从此以后,这里就成了"自古华山不纳粮"的宝地,而且这个经典的象棋残局也得以流传。

● 华山下棋亭(图片提供:微图)
Chess Pavilion of Huashan Mountain

Emperor Taizu of the Song Dynasty Played Chinese Chess

Legend has it that Emperor Taizu of the Song Dynasty (Zhao Kuangyin) was obsessed with Chinese chess and had rarely failed one set of the game due to his excellent skills. So he believed that he was invincible in the game. Before his coronation, Zhao Kuangyin travelled around the country. One day, he arrived at the territory of Huashan Mountain and was told that there was a chess master named Chen Tuan on the mountain. So he went to find him and asked him to play a set of Chinese chess together. Chen Tuan assumed Zhao Kuangyin might be the emperor in future so he made a joke with him. Chen showed weakness on purpose (Zhao-black side and Chen-red side). When Zhao felt the coming victory, Chen said: "If I won, you must grant me the Huashan Mountain when you conquered the whole country." However, Zhao didn't think he could be emperor or would lose this game. So he instantly made the promise to him. Unexpectedly, after several rounds, Zhao's pieces were taken down by Chen's horse. He was astonished and admitted the defeat. Later, when Zhao Kuangyin ascended the throne, he kept his promise and eliminated the taxes in this area. Since then, Huashan area earned its fame as a place without the taxes and this game also became a legend.

继宋代之后，象棋在元明时期又有了大的发展。尤其是明代中期以后，象棋的发展进入了一个新的阶段。杨慎、唐寅、袁枚等文人学者都爱好下象棋，大批著名棋手的涌现，显示了象棋受到社会各阶层民众喜爱的状况。明代最出名的棋手是李开先（1502—1568），他既是以戏曲《宝剑记》享誉文坛的戏剧家，又是当时象棋界首屈一指的高手。他在《送棋客吴橘隐兼及吴升甫》一诗中写道："虽云国手同推汝，叵奈强兵独有吾。每让三

the Chinese chess today. In the Southern Song Dynasty, the Chinese chess became a very popular board game which was obsessive to many celebrities including Li Qingzhao, Liu Kezhuang, Hong Zun, Wen Tianxiang and other literati. Half of the "Chess Attendants" served in the courtyard specialized Chinese chess. Among the common people, there appeared the professional Chinese chess player called "chess master" and the craftsman producing chess pieces and boards. Several canons were also written in the Southern Song Dynasty,

先难成埒，纵饶一马亦长输。"大意为，虽然你们都是公认的象棋国手，怎奈遇到我这个高手。即使被我让三先（让对方第一步，连走三着棋），也不是我的对手；让一马也赢不了一两局。吴橘隐和吴升甫这些当时著名的棋手都败在李开先手下。嘉靖前后，出现了两部象棋巨著。一部是《梦入神机》，一部是《适情雅趣》。《梦入神机》全书共十卷，所收的残局在700局左右，在数量上堪称古代棋谱之王。隆庆四年（1570）刊印的《适情雅趣》，共收棋局550局，被认为是一部象棋的"杀法大全"，一直为后

such as *Theory of Chinese Chess* by Hong Mai, *Collection of Best Chinese Chess Strategies* by Ye Maoqing and *General Records of All Things* by Chen Yuanliang.

After the Song Dynasty, Chinese chess gained further development in the Yuan and Ming dynasties. Especially after the middle age of Ming Dynasty, Chinese chess entered another brand new phase. Then, many celebrities like Yang Shen, Tang Yin, Yuan Mei and other literati were all fond of playing Chinese chess. Abundant famous players appeared, which reflected the prevalence of this game. The most prestigious master in the Ming Dynasty was Li Kaixian

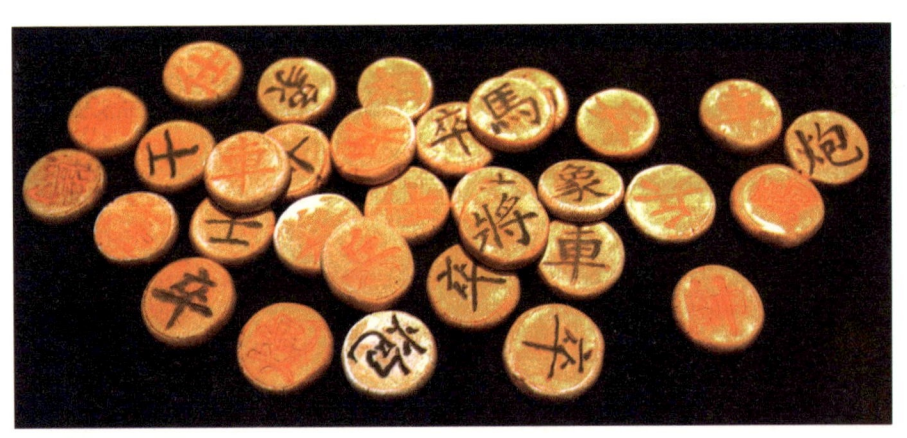

• 陶制象棋子（明）
Porcelain Chinese Chess Pieces (Ming Dynasty, 1368-1644)

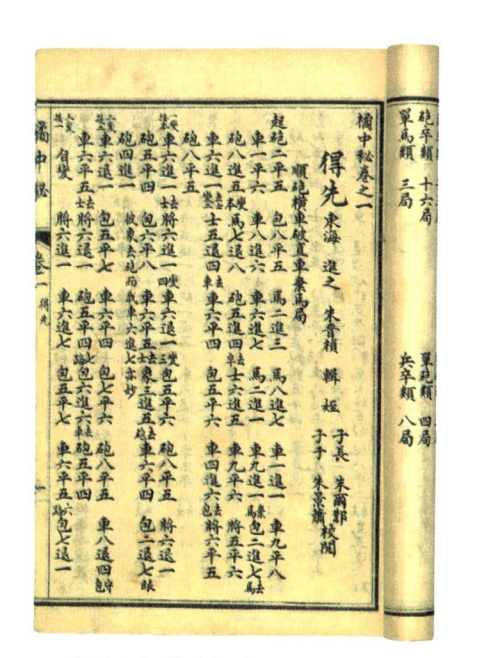

《橘中秘》棋谱书影
Photo Image of *Secret in the Orange*

代棋家所推崇。明代象棋谱中名气最大的是崇祯五年（1632）刊印的《橘中秘》。全书共四卷，内容大多选自《适情雅趣》，经过精心整理，篇幅不大，实用性很强，因而问世以后颇受欢迎，直至今天仍拥有众多的读者。

清代前期，社会稳定，经济发展，为象棋活动的发展提供了良好的环境。康熙至嘉庆年间，涌现出不少高超的棋手。康熙年间著名的围棋大国手徐星友同时也是一位象

(1502-1568), who was a screenwriter famous for *Story of Treasured Sword* and also a top master in Chinese chess. In his poem *Seeing off the Guests Wu Juyin and Wu Shengfu*, he wrote that: "Although you two are the national players, unfortunately, your opponent is me; Even if I let you move three rounds ahead of me, you cannot beat me either; Even if I only use one horse piece, you still cannot beat me." Wu Juyin and Wu Shengfu were famous masters in Chinese chess, however, all of them were defeated by Li Kaixian. Around Jiajing Period, there appeared two canons about Chinese chess: *Secret Strategies in Dreams* and *Recreation Hobbies*. The *Secret Strategies in Dreams* with ten volumes includes more than 700 sets of games, which deserves the title of the King of Ancient Annotations. Published in 1570 A.D., the book *Recreation Hobbies* which includes 550 sets of games is considered as the "Attack Canon of Chinese Chess" and has earned the praise of the chess players in later generations. The most famous chess note in the Ming Dynasty is the *Secret in the Orange* published in 1632 A.D., with four volumes and the content mostly quoted from *Recreation Hobbies* after meticulous arrangement.

橘中秘

明代象棋名谱《橘中秘》的书名来自一个玄幻传说。据唐代牛僧孺的《玄怪录》记载，四川巴州地区的一户人家有个橘园，一年深秋橘子都已成熟收获后，树上只余下两个大橘，有人头般大小。人们将其摘下剖开一看，不见橘瓤，每个橘子里都有两个老人在下象棋，各有胜负。后来人们就以"橘中之乐"作为象棋的别称。

Secret in the Orange

The famous Chinese chess note *Secret in the Orange* in the Ming Dynasty got its name from a legendary tale. According to the *Notes of Mysterious Things* written by Niu Sengru in the Tang Dynasty, there was a orangery belonged to a household in Bazhou area, Sichuan Province. One year, after the harvest of the oranges, there were only two oranges left hanging on the tree as big as human's head. People picked them and cut them open. Surprisingly, there was no orange flesh inside instead of two old men playing Chinese chess in each orange. So later, people use the term "Joy in the Orange" as the alternative name of Chinese chess.

• 玛瑙雕"橘中二叟"
Agate Sculpture of Two Old Men in the Orange

棋高手。据记载："钱塘徐星友，长于弈（围棋），尤擅象戏，遨游燕赵齐鲁间，尽败当地诸名手，有钱塘双绝之誉云。"这说明徐星友的象棋水平甚至不低于他的围棋造诣。徐星友在康熙末年被青年棋手程兰如击败，程兰如也是一位围棋、象棋兼通的名家。据《扬州画舫录》记载："程兰如弈棋不如施（定庵）、范（西屏），而象棋称国手。"康熙至嘉庆年间，诞生了

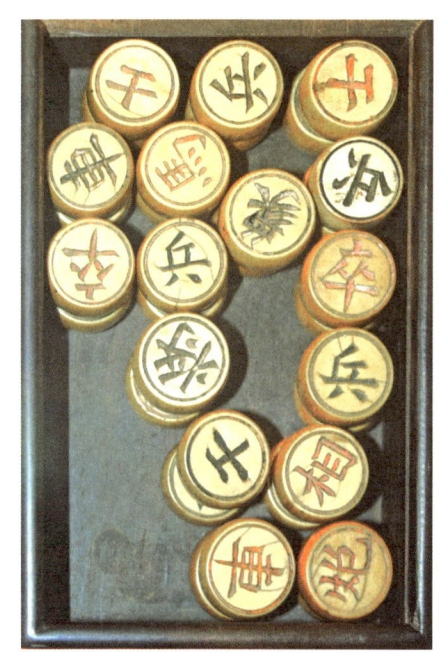

- 象牙制象棋子（清）
  Ivory Chinese Chess Pieces (Qing Dynasty, 1616-1911)

Although being short, this book is with strong practical applicability, so it earns people's favor and still gets many readers.

In the early period of Qing Dynasty, the stability of political situation and development of economy built a healthy environment for the spread of Chinese chess. During the Kangxi Period and Jiaqing Period, there appeared many top players. The famous chess master of the game Go, Xu Xingyou also was a top player in Chinese chess. According to the records: "Xu Xingyou from Qiantang City excelled in the game Go, as well as Chinese chess. He travelled across country and beat all the local masters, hence got the name Top hand from Qiantang." It indicates Xu got same talent in Chinese chess. In the late Kangxi Period, he was defeated by a young player named Cheng Rulan. Cheng was also a player specializing in both Go and Chinese chess. According to the record in *Travelling Records of Yangzhou*: "Although Cheng Rulan's skill in Go was not as good as other players such as Shi Ding'an and Fan Xiping, his talent in Chinese chess was unparalleled." During the Kangxi Period and Jiaqing Period, there appeared abundant books about Chinese chess. Among them, the most

- 20世纪30年代的人体象棋游戏
  Live-action Chinese Chess Game in 1930s

一批象棋著作，其中最著名的是抄本全局谱《梅花谱》。《梅花谱》是康熙年间的棋手王再越所著，棋局变化细致，着法精彩，在象棋界影响深广。从嘉庆以后，象棋活动显出了颓势，进入了一段"沉寂期"。这一时期，尽管实战水平仍有一定程度的提高，但高质量的棋谱再也没有出现。

直到中华人民共和国成立后，象棋进入了一个崭新的发展阶段。1956年，象棋成为国家体育项目，几乎每年都举行全国性的比赛。50多年来，在众多棋类活动和比赛的推动下，象棋棋艺水平提高得很快，优秀棋手不断涌现。

famous canon is the chess annotation *Note of Plum Blossom* written by Wang Zaiyue a Chinese chess player in Kangxi Period. This book includes series of excellent sets of games with delicate pieces' layout and many variations, which has exerted great influence on Chinese chess. After Jiaqing Period, Chinese chess lost its momentum and entered a declining phase during which, although strategies were continuously developed, no more chess annotations with high-quality ever appeared.

After the establishment of the People's Republic of China in 1949, Chinese chess entered a new stage of development. In 1956, it was included as the National Sports Event. Each year, there would be the national competition of Chinese chess. Over the past 50 years, due to the promotion of many other board games and competitions, the strategy of Chinese chess has developed rapidly along with the appearance of many excellent players.

> 象棋的棋具与规则

象棋的棋具包括棋盘与棋子，由两人轮流走子，以"将死"或"困毙"对方的将（帅）为胜。

象棋的棋盘

棋盘是长方形的平面，由九条平行的竖线和十条平行的横线相交组成，共有九十个交叉点，棋子就摆在交叉点上。中间部分，也就是棋盘的第五、第六

> Sets and Rules of Chinese Chess

The sets of Chinese chess include the board and pieces. The two players should take their turns to make the move to try to "take" or "besiege" opponent's Lord.

Board of Chinese Chess

The board of Chinese chess is a flat rectangle plane with nine parallel vertical lines and ten parallel horizontal lines crossing with each other to create total 90 intersections on

• 木质象棋棋桌
Wooden Board of Chinese Chess

河界
River Border

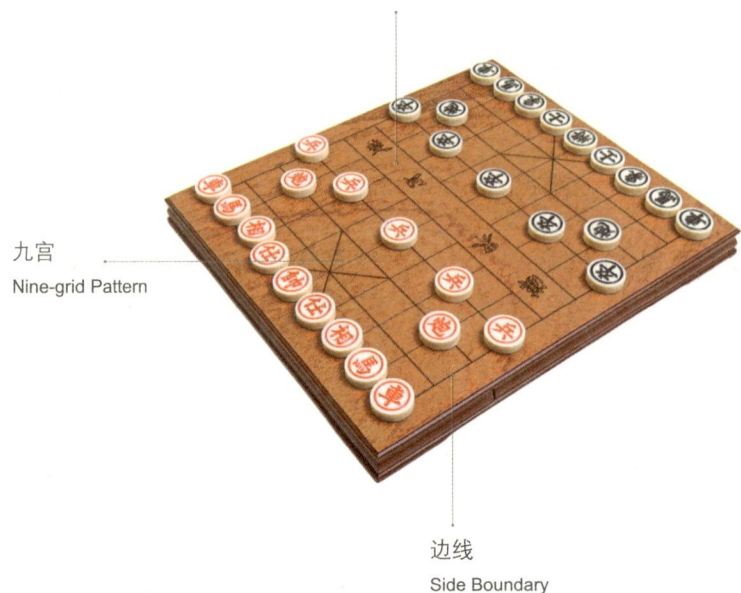

九宫
Nine-grid Pattern

边线
Side Boundary

- 象棋的棋盘与棋子
  Board of Chinese Chess

两横线之间未画竖线的空白地带称为"楚河汉界",简称"河界"。两端的中间,也就是两端第四条到第六条竖线之间的正方形部位,以斜交叉线构成"米"字方格的地方,叫作"九宫"。

which the chess pieces are placed. In the middle of the board (the area between the 5th and 6th horizontal lines), there is the "Chu River and Han Boundaries", or "River Border" for short. In the middle part at the ends of two sides (the areas between the 4th and 6th vertical lines), there are two checks consisting of two cross oblique lines, called "Nine-grid Pattern".

棋盘上的"楚河汉界"

"楚河汉界"指的是河南省荥阳市黄河南岸广武山上的鸿沟。沟口宽约800米,深达200米,是古代的一处军事要地。西汉初年楚汉相争时,汉高祖刘邦和西楚霸王项羽仅在荥阳一带就爆发了"大战七十,小战四十",因种种原因,项羽"乃与汉约,中分天下,割鸿沟以西为汉,以东为楚",鸿沟便成了楚汉的边界。如今鸿沟两边还有当年两军对垒的城址,东边是霸王城,西边是汉王城。

"Chu River and Han Boundaries" in the Board of Chinese Chess

Chu River and Han's Boundaries indicate the chasm on Guangwu Mountain on the south bank of Yellow River in Xingyang City, Henan Province. The chasm is with a width of 800 m and depth of 200 m, which was a crucial military position in ancient times. In the Battle between Chu and Han in the early Western Han Dynasty (206 B.C.-25 A.D.), Liu Bang, the future Emperor Gaozu of the Han Dynasty and the Overlord Xiang Yu of the Westen Chu broke out "70 big battles and 40 small conflicts" in this area. Due to several reasons, Xiang Yu "made a compromise to rule the country with Liu Bang and took the chasm as the border of Han Dynasty (west) and Chu Dynasty (east)". Since then the chasm became the official border of the two authorities. Nowadays, there are the ruins of fortresses at that time. To the east is the City of the Overlord, and to the west is the City of the King of Han.

象棋的棋子

象棋的棋子一共有32枚,分为红、黑两方,下棋时遵循"红先黑后"的惯例。

帅(将)

红方为"帅",黑方为"将"。

帅和将是棋中的首脑,是双方竭力争夺的目标。它只能在"九宫"之内活动,可上可下,可左可

Pieces of Chinese Chess

There are total 32 pieces in Chinese chess game, with two colors: red and black. In the game, the players should obey the rule of "Red First".

Lord (General)

Red side is carved with "帅" (*Shuai*, Lord) and black side is carved with "将" (*Jiang*, General).

The pieces of lord and general are the

右，每次走动只能按竖线或横线走动一格。帅与将不能在同一直线上直接对面，否则后走一方判负。

仕（士）

仕（士）是帅（将）的贴身保镖，也只能在九宫内走动。它的行棋路径只能是九宫内的斜线。

象（相）

红方为"相"，黑方为"象"。

象（相）的主要作用是保护自己的帅（将）。它的走法是每次循对角线走两格，就像走过一个"田"字，俗称"象飞田"。其活动范围限于本方阵地，且如果"田"字中央有棋子就不能走，俗称"塞象眼"。

车（車）

车无论横线、竖线均可行走，只要无子阻拦，步数不受限制。因此，一车可以控制17个点，有"一车十子寒"之称。

炮（砲）

炮走动与车完全相同，但在吃子时必须跳过一个棋子，俗称"炮打隔子"。

leader of the game and also the ultimate targets for both sides. It can only move within the "Nine-grid Pattern", turning up and down or left and right. Each turn, it can only take one step along the vertical or horizontal lines. The pieces of lord and general can not be placed face to face. Otherwise, the last one who takes the move will be considered being defeated directly.

Guard (Soldier)

The piece of guard is lord (general)'s close bodyguard, which only can move within the Nine-grid Pattern as well. It should move along the oblique lines.

Elephant (Minister)

Red side is carved with " 相 " (*Xiang*, Minister) and black side is carved with " 象 " (*Xiang*, Elephant).

The piece of minister (elephant) should protect their own lord (general). Each turn, it can move across two grids with an oblique track. As its moving track looks like the character " 田 " (*Tian*), so there is a saying called "Elephant with the Flying Pattern of 田 ". And it can not move across the river border and also can not take the step if there is a piece standing in the center of the moving track, which is called "blocking elephant's eye".

- 帅和将

  Pieces of Lord and General

- 仕和士

  Pieces of Two Kinds of Guards Carved with 仕 and 士

- 士（仕）的走法

  Moving Track of the Piece of Guard

- 象（相）的走法——"象飞田"

  Moving Track of the Piece of Elephant: "Elephant with the Flying Pattern of 田"

- 横行无阻的车

一般认为象棋开局快速出车至关重要，民间棋谚有云："三步不出车，满盘皆是输。"

Dashing Chariot

Generally, it is believed that it is key point that the player should move its chariot pieces once the game begins, which is said as: "Not moving chariot within three rounds makes a defeat."

- 炮打隔子

Cannon Only Hit the Second One

- 古代战车示意图

Ancient Chariot

马

马的走法是先横着或直着走一格，然后再斜着走一条对角线，就像走过一个"日"字，俗称"马

- 马的走法——"马走日"
图中黑棋马可以一步吃掉红棋炮。
Moving Track of the Piece of Horse: "Horse with the Moving Pattern of 日"
The black horse can take red cannon in one more.

- 别马腿
Spraining the Horse Leg

Chariot

The piece of chariot can move across the board freely along the horizontal and vertical lines, as long as there is no piece standing in its way. It can move any steps without limitation. Therefore, one chariot can cover 17 points, hence the saying "one chariot can rival ten pieces".

Cannon

The moving pattern of the piece of cannon is exact same with the piece of chariot. However, when taking opponent's pieces, the cannon must jump over one piece, which is called "the cannon only hit the second one".

Horse

The moving track of the piece of horse is to move horizontally or vertically first and then go along the diagonal line. As its track looks like a character "日" (Ri), so this moving pattern is also called "horse with the moving pattern of 日". If there is a piece standing in

• 兵与卒
Pieces of Two Kinds of Pawns Carved with 兵 and 卒

走日"。如果在要去的方向有棋子挡住，马就无法走过去，俗称"别马腿"。

兵（卒）

红方为"兵"，黑方为"卒"。

兵（卒）只能向前，不能后退。在未过河前，不能左、右移动。过河以后可左、右移动，但也只能一次一步。

行棋规则

对局时，由执红棋的一方先走，双方轮流各走一着，直至分出胜、负、和，对局即终了。轮到走棋的一方，要将某个棋子从一个交

its way, the horse can not take the step, which is called "spraining the horse leg".

Pawn

Red side is carved with "兵" (Bing, Pawn) and black side is carved with "卒" (Zu, Pawn).

The piece of pawn should only move forward one step in each turn before it goes across the river border. It can not move backward in their own territory. After stepping across the river border, the pawn can move left or right and take one step in each turn as well.

Rules of Chinese Chess

In the game, the red side takes the first step and then the two players take turns

叉点走到另一个交叉点，或者吃掉对方的棋子而占领其交叉点，都算走一着。双方各走一着，称为一个回合。

对局中，出现下列情况之一，本方算输，对方赢：

1. 本方的帅（将）被对方棋子吃掉；

2. 本方发出认输请求；

3. 本方走棋超出步时限制。

moving their pieces until the game reaches its result of three situations including win, fail and tie. In each turn, both of them can move one of their pieces from one intersection to another or just take out the opponent's piece and occupy its location. Both of the sides finishing one step is called one round.

In the game, if any of following situation appears, the home side will lose and the opponent will win:

1. The piece of lord (general) of the home side is taken by the opponent;

2. The home side admits defeat;

3. The home side doesn't take its step within the time limit.

- 马后炮

在象棋中，马后炮是一种基本杀法。攻一方的马与对方的将帅处于同一直线或同一横线，中间隔一步，再用炮在马后将军。

Cannon behind the Horse

In Chinese chess, the attack strategy of cannon behind the horse is a basic approach. The attacker moves the horse to the same line of the opponent's lord (general) and in the next turn, uses the cannon behind the horse to take over the lord (general).

- 当头炮

当头炮是一种十分常见的象棋开局着法，即把炮放在正中线位，威胁对方将（帅），是先走一方采取主动攻势的一种布局。许多象棋大师总结，在对弈中先手走当头炮占有一定优势。

Head-on Cannon

The head-on cannon is a very common opening strategy, which is to move the piece of cannon to the midcourt line to threat the opponent's general (lord). It is an active approach. Many chess masters conclude that the strategy of head-on cannon has an advantage over the game.

- 双炮将

双炮将是一种象棋杀法，即用一只炮作炮架，另一只炮将军，或一炮在前将军，一炮在后控制，从而形成双炮将。

Double-cannon Checkmate

The double-cannon checkmate is an attack in Chinese chess. It is to use one cannon as the gun carriage and the other cannon to hit the lord (general); or use one cannon to take out the lord (general) and the other cannon as backup to form the double-cannon checkmake.

- 双车错

双车错是象棋最为实用、简捷的杀法之一，即由一只车控制九宫的纵向或横向中路，另一只车在通过控制纵向或横向边路将死对方。因为此法太过实用，也容易被对手看出，所以在高水平对战中并不常见。

Double-chariot Attack

The double-chariot attack is one of the most practical and common attack strategies, which is to use one chariot to cover the vertical or horizontal middle route and the other chariot to cover the side route in order to take over the opponent's lord (general). As it is too convenient, so the strategy can be easily exposed. Therefore, it is rarely seen in the game among the skillful players.

棋局之王——七星聚会

"七星聚会"是从清代起广泛流传于民间的象棋"四大名局"之一，清代刊行的著名棋谱中几乎都收录此局，只是名称略有差异。这局棋由红、黑双方各七子组成，结局时双方多合计七子，故而得名"七星"。七星聚会的构思精巧，陷阱四伏，乍看之下红方似有胜机，但求胜心切者往往会误中圈套。这个著名排局长期在民间流传，有多种变着，素来被誉为"残局之王"。

King of the Composition of Chinese Chess: Get-together of Seven Stars

Get-together of Seven Stars indicates one of the "Four Great Chinese Chess Compositions" in the Qing Dynasty (1616-1911). Almost all the famous chess annotations published in the Qing Dynasty included this composition, only with different names. As this set consists seven pieces from each side (total 14 pieces) and it will leave seven pieces in all at the end, so this composition is called "Seven Stars". It is with delicate strategy and complicated traps. At the first sight, the red side seems to be able to win the game. However, the competitive and confident player might fall in the trap if not being cautious. As this famous composition has been well known to the people for a long time and has numerous variants, so it is also called the "King of Remain Game ".

- 残局之王 "七星聚会"
  King of the Composition of Chinese Chess: "Get-together of Seven Stars "

> 象棋与传统诗画

历史上许多文人墨客都爱下象棋，以象棋为主题吟诗作画，留下许多传世佳作。

唐代诗人白居易在爱好围棋的同时，对象棋也颇为着迷。他曾写下"兵冲象戏车"的诗句，提到了象棋中的"兵"和"车"的对局片段。

北宋徽宗赵佶在《宣和宫词》中写道："白檀象戏小盘平，牙子金书字更明。"大意是白檀木制成的象棋棋盘光滑平整，象牙制成的棋子上刻以鎏金的字，显得格外分明。体现出北宋宫廷中象棋棋具的精致和奢华。

明代著名学者王守仁小时候对象棋非常痴迷，经常下象棋下到忘记吃饭。有一次到了用餐时间，王

> Chinese Chess and Traditional Chinese Poetry and Painting

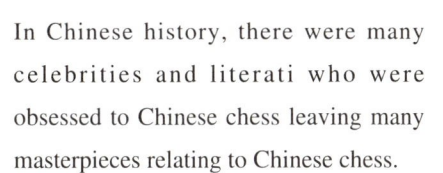

In Chinese history, there were many celebrities and literati who were obsessed to Chinese chess leaving many masterpieces relating to Chinese chess.

Despite the addiction to the game Go, the famous poet Bai Juyi in the Tang Dynasty was also fond of Chinese chess. He once wrote the verses "pawn is dashing toward the chariot in a game of Chinese chess", in which he mentioned a segment of Chinese chess including "pawn" and "chariot".

Zhao Ji, Emperor Huizong of the Northern Song Dynasty once wrote in the *Imperial Verses in Xuanhe Period*: "The Chinese chess board made from symplocos paniculata is flat and smooth; and the ivory chess pieces are carved with gilded characters." It reflects the

守仁的母亲到处找他吃饭都找不到，最后终于在河边找到与人下棋的儿子，一气之下将象棋都扔到了河里。王守仁眼看着心爱的棋子沉入河底，非常悲伤，于是写下一首《哭象棋》："象棋在手乐悠悠，苦被严亲一旦丢。兵卒堕河皆不救，将军溺水一齐休。马行千里随波去，士入三川逐浪流。炮声一响天地震，象若心头为人揪。"整首诗里，所有的棋子仿佛成了诗人统率的一支兵马，"兵卒堕河"，

王守仁像
Portrait of Wang Shouren

extremely exquisite and luxurious set of Chinese chess in the courtyard of the Northern Song Dynasty.

In the Ming Dynasty, the famous scholar Wang Shouren was obsessed with Chinese chess and often forgot to have meals. One day at mealtime, his mother could not find him anywhere until ran into Wang by the riverside while he was playing Chinese chess with others. She was so angry that she threw his board and pieces into the river. Watching his beloved chess pieces sinking into the water, Wang was really upside and wrote a poem named *Crying for Chinese Chess*, as quoted: "Happily I held my chess pieces, which suddenly were threw away by my mother. The pawns are falling into the river, as well as the lord and general. The horse rides along the waves and the guard also dashes into the river. The cannon fires with loud sound, and the elephant makes me worried the most." In this poem, he vividly depicts all the chess pieces as his army. The picture of "falling pawns", "drowned lord and general", "running horse" and "dashing guards" is full of a child's innocence interest and also fully conveys the author's grieve.

The famous scholar Yuan Mei in

• 王守仁故居
Former Residence of Wang Shouren

"将军溺水","马随波去","士逐浪流"。整首诗淋漓尽致地表达了他失去象棋的悲伤之情,传达出生动的童真与童趣。

清代文学家袁枚也曾写过一首诗,描绘了象棋对局者全神贯注,时而欣喜时而焦急的心态:"拢袖观棋有所思,分明楚汉两举时。非常喜欢非常恼,不看棋人总不知。"(拢起袖子静静地观看别人

the Qing Dynasty once wrote a poem depicting the concentrated expression of the players and their mental activities: "Roll up sleeves and watch the game while pondering, clearly it is the confrontation of the armies of Chu and Han. The mental state of chess fans that is sometimes joyful and sometimes anxious can not be fathomed by the outsiders."

Among the Chinese paintings with the theme of Chinese chess, the *Emperor*

下棋若有所思，下棋的双方分明就是楚汉两军对峙。棋迷这种有时欢欣有时焦虑的心理状态，不看棋的人是体会不到的。）

在以象棋为题材的古代绘画中，以南宋画家萧照的《中兴瑞应图》最负盛名。这幅长卷共分三段，其中第一段画的是树木茂盛的深宫内庭，台榭中设有棋盘，几位女眷立在一侧，一位着红袍的贵妇作掷棋子状。据画前的题赞得知，穿红袍的女人是南宋开国皇帝赵构

Gaozong's Ascending to the Throne, by Xiao Zhao in the Southern Song Dynasty is of the highest reputation. This scroll has three parts: one depicts the inner courtyard with flourishing plants and a lady in red robe moving chess piece in a pavilion who is surrounded by several standing maids. According to the postscripts, the lady in red robe is Empress Xianren, mother of Emperor Gaozong, Zhao Gou (founder of the Southern Song Dynasty). While taking a close look, the audience can find that

- 《临萧照中兴瑞应图》仇英（明）【局部】
  这是明代画家仇英临摹萧照原作的作品，图中建筑的比例、形象、风格及细部都极其忠实于原作。

  Chinese Painting: *Imitating Work of Emperor Gaozong's Ascending to the Throne*, by Qiu Ying (Ming Dynasty, 1368-1644) [Part]

  It is a imitating work of Xiao Zhao's famous painting by Qiu Ying in the Ming Dynasty, in which the scale of the architecture, appearance, style, as well as the detailed parts are true to the original one.

的母亲显仁皇后。细看桌上的棋盘，果然写有赵构名字的棋子落入九宫格中，而写其他皇子姓名的棋子都在其外，喻示赵构即位是顺应天意，众愿所归。

Zhao Gou's name is positioned inside the Nine-grid Pattern, while others' are scattered outside. This indicates that Zhao Gou is the legitimate emperor granted by the heaven.

象棋谚语
Idioms Relating to Chinese Chess

流传至今的象棋谚语不仅是历代象棋爱好者经验的总结，而且体现了民间语言的精妙，蕴含着很深的人生智慧。

The Chinese chess phrases and expressions are not only the conclusion of the Chinese chess enthusiasts' experience but also the reflection of the exquisiteness of folk language and the wisdom of life.

象棋性质：
象棋似布阵，点子如点兵。

Nature of Chinese Chess:
Playing Chinese chess resembles leading an army, and moving pieces resembles deploying soldiers.

争先原则：
兵贵神速，抢先入局。
宁失一马，不失一先。

Principles of Being Competitive:
Speed is the key, and take the initiative with the first attack.
Rather lose one Horse, than lose the advantage.

求稳原则：

临杀勿急，稳中取胜。

一招不慎，满盘皆输。

Principle of Being Calm:
Do not hurry in taking pieces, and keeping calm shall lead to victory.
One false move may cost you the whole game.

棋子威力：

马跳连环不用车。

老将出马，一个顶俩。

开局炮胜马，残局马胜炮。

Power of Chess Pieces:
Horse can jump without the help of the Chariot.
The Lord (General) can rival two other pieces.
Cannon is better than the Horse in the opening, and the Horse is better than the Cannon in the closing.

对局艺德：

观棋不语真君子，落子不悔大丈夫。

Moral in Chinese Chess Playing:
True gentleman should never talk while watching the game; real man should never regret his move.

输赢心态：

得意之时休大意，小卒过河亦英雄。

棋是木头块，输了再重摆。

Mental Activities about Failure and Win:
Be cautious while in a smooth going, and be proud while moving the Pawn across the River Border.
Chinese chess pieces are wood blocks actually, so do not fuss about the gain and loss.

其他棋艺
Other Board Games

  除了围棋和象棋这两大棋艺之外，中国古代还曾流行过六博、塞戏、弹棋、双陆等其他棋艺。许多少数民族也有各自的传统棋类，是中国棋艺大家族中不可缺少的组成部分。

Aside from Chinese chess and the game of Go, there were other popular board games in ancient China, including Liubo, Saixi, Tanqi, Shuanglu (also known as backgammon), etc. Many ethnic groups also have their own traditional board games, which consist of an essential part of board games in China.

> 六博

六博，又作"陆博""博"，是中国古代一种掷采行棋的博戏，因使用6根博箸而得名。其玩法是以杀掉特定棋子为胜，所以有人推论象棋类游戏可能从六博演变而来。

六博的源流

六博，大约出现在春秋时期，到了战国时期已相当流行。楚国人宋玉所作的《楚辞·招魂》中有云："菎蔽象棋，有六簙些。分曹并进，遒相迫些。"反映出战国前后六博棋在荆楚一带流行的情况。成书于西汉的《史记·苏秦列传》中描写了战国时齐国都城临淄繁荣的情况，提到当地人在进行"斗鸡走狗，六博蹴鞠"等娱乐活动，也表明六博在当时已相当普及。

> Liubo

Liubo, also known as "Lubo" or "Bo", is an ancient Chinese board game played by the throw of six sticks as dice. As the game allows its player's piece to kill the specific piece to win, so some Chinese scholars infer that Chinese chess was based on it.

Origin of Liubo

Liubo, also known as Bo, was known to be invented around the Spring and Autumn Period (770 B.C.-476 B.C.) and became a popular game in the Warring States Period (475 B.C.-221 B.C.). For example, the game is described in the poem *Summons of the Soul* written by Song Yu from the State of Chu: "With jade chess pieces, each side holds 6 pieces. sides are taken; They advance together; keenly they threaten each other." It reflected the popularity of

• 绿釉陶六博俑（汉）
Green Glazed Clay Figurines Playing Liubo (Han Dynasty, 206 B.C.-220 A.D.)

秦汉时期，六博得到更加广泛的传播，从宫廷贵族、官僚文士到普通百姓都乐于此道，还出现了一些与六博相关的有趣故事。据西汉人刘向编撰的《说苑·正谏篇》记载，战国末年秦国的佞臣长信侯嫪毐，因为秦王嬴政年纪尚轻，又仗着太后的崇信，经常以太上皇自居。在秦王嬴政成年行冠礼的宴会上，嫪毐设六博助兴，在博局中口出狂言，惹恼了秦王，最后被满门抄斩。

Liubo in ancient Jingchu area (now around Hubei Province). According to *Biography of Su Qin* in *Records of the Grand Historian*, the capital city of Linzi was so prosperous that its citizens were all able to indulge in activities such as "cock fighting, dog racing, playing Liubo and playing kick ball", which also indicated Liubo was widely known by the public at that time.

In the Qin and Han dynasties, Liubo gained even wider popularity among the ruling clan, aristocrats, government officials, literati, and ordinary people. There were also anecdotes about Liubo. According to *Zhengjian Pian* (*Admonish*) in *Shuo Yuan* (*Garden of Stories*), the Duke of Changxin Lao Ai, a vicious courtier of the State of Qin during the late Warring States Period imposed him as the step-father of the young King (Ying Zheng) due to the trust of the Ying Zheng's mother. On the banquet to celebrate the Adulthood Capping Ceremony, Lao Ai set Liubo games to play with the guests and bragged about himself, which infuriated the King and was killed later together with all his family.

During the reign of the Emperor Jing of the Western Han Dynasty,

• 仙人六博图画像石拓片（汉）

这幅作品出土于成都市郊，图中两位仙人肩披羽饰，相对六博，背景有仙草、凤鸟为陪衬。当时把六博看成是神仙的娱乐，可见六博在当时影响之深。

Stone Rubbing of Immortals Playing Liubo (Han Dynasty, 206 B.C.-220 A.D.)

This stone rubbing was unearthed from the suburbs of Chengdu. The two immortals have feather decorations on their shoulders and are surrounded by magic flowers and a phoenix. The depiction of Liubo as a game of the immortals showed its deep influence on the society.

西汉景帝时，以吴、楚两国为首的七个诸侯国发起叛乱，被称为"七国之乱"，据说起因就与六博不无关系。景帝做太子时十分喜好六博，一次同吴王刘濞的儿子下棋时发生了口角，他竟举起博局砸向吴王的儿子。从此吴王刘濞怀恨在心，到景帝登基的第三年，吴国联合楚、赵诸王举兵。这些事件都反

seven attached states started a revolt leading by the Principality of Wu and the Principality of Chu, known as the "Rebellion of the Seven States". It was said that one of the causes was related with Liubo. While Emperor Jing was the Crown Prince, he enjoyed playing Liubo. Once, he competed with the heir of Liu Bi who was the prince of the Principality of Wu in a Liubo game. During

• 铜六博棋盘（西汉）（图片提供：FOTOE）
Copper Liubo Board (Western Han Dynasty, 206 B.C.-25 A.D.)

映出汉代贵族阶层好为六博的风尚。

《西京杂记》中曾记载，当时有个叫许博昌的安陵人，擅长六博，曾创编了一套六博的棋术口诀，后来又作《六博经》一篇，受到许多人的欢迎。他的口诀连小孩子都能随口背出，可见六博在民间受欢迎的程度。六博的盛行一直延续到三国时期。

六博最初是一种娱乐活动，后来甚至演变成一种博奕手段。六博

arguments over the game, the Crown Prince threw the Liubo board at Liu Bi's son. Liu Bi thus had great hatred for the emperor. In the third year of the Emperor Jing's reign, the Principality of Wu started the revolt with other princes, including the Principality of Chu and the Principality of Zhao. These events reflected the popularity of Liubo among the aristocracy lived in the Han Dynasty (206 B.C.-220 A.D.).

According to *Miscellany of the Western Capital*, Xu Bochang from Anling was good at playing Liubo, created a series of pithy formulas about it, and later wrote a paper named *Liubo Jing* (*Book of Liubo*) which became an instant hit. Some of his formulas could even be remembered by kids, showing the popularity of Liubo among the people. This game kept its momentum until the Three Kingdoms Period (220-280).

Initially, Liubo was an entertainment, but it was even involved into a strategic

在汉代以后逐渐呈现出衰势，进入晋代后便销声匿迹了。

棋具与规则

20世纪70年代中期，湖北云梦睡虎地的秦墓中出土了六博棋局。棋局接近方形，长32厘米、宽29厘米、高2厘米，局面阴刻道纹、方框和4个圆点。同时出土的还有漆黑的

- **渔猎博局镜（东汉）**
  博局镜又名"规矩镜"，是汉代铜镜发展中流行时间最长的一种镜式。镜背规则的装饰方式实际上是古代六博的棋格。

  Fishing and Hunting Mirror with Liubo Board Pattern (Eastern Han Dynasty, 25-220)

  Liubo mirror, also known as "board mirror", was a type of bronze mirror that has been popular for a long time during the development of bronze mirrors in the Han Dynasty (206 B.C.-220 A.D.). The decoration pattern on its back was actually Liubo board used in ancient China.

maneuver. Hence, after the end of the Han Dynasty (206 B.C.-220 A.D.), Liubo gradually lost its popularity and there were no known descriptions of Liubo in the Jin Dynasty (265-420).

Equipment and Rules

In the middle of the 1970s, a set of Liubo equipment was excavated from a tomb built in the Qin Dynasty (221 B.C.-206 B.C.) at Shuihudi in Yunmeng County, Hubei Province. The board was nearly in a square shape with a size of 32 cm by 29 cm by 2 cm. It was carved in intaglio with stripes, squares, and four dots. 12 dark-lacquered pieces with 6 rectangle ones and 6 square ones were unearthed simultaneously. There were also six sticks with the length about 23.5 cm that were made of halved thin bamboo sticks and filled with metal powders. Thus, a complete set of Liubo may include the board, the game pieces, and the sticks (later known as dice). Besides, there were tokens to record the progress of the game.

There were two variants of Liubo, "Dabo" (Greater Bo) and "Xiaobo" (Lesser Bo). "Dabo" was used during and before the Western Han Dynasty (206 B.C.-25 A.D.). The players would place

棋子12颗，6颗为长方形，另6颗为方形；并有用半边细竹管填以金属粉制成的"箸"，共6根，长约23.5厘米。可以看出，一套完整的六博棋，应包括棋局、棋子、箸(即后世所称的骰子)。另外还有博筹，用于记录输赢情况。

六博的行棋方法主要包括"大博"和"小博"两种。西汉时及以前的博法为"大博"，对博的双方各在己方棋盘的曲道上排列好6枚棋子，其中1枚代表"枭"，5枚称作"散"，以"枭"为大。对博时，双方先轮流掷箸，根据掷得的数量多少来行棋。行棋时双方互相逼迫，"枭"要努力吃掉对方的"散"，同时在己方"散"的配合下调兵遣将，争取时机杀掉对方的"枭"。对博的胜负以杀"枭"来决定。

东汉时期，六博的形制发生变革，出现了二"茕"（与箸的作用一样）的"小博"。一方执6枚白棋，一方执6枚黑棋，双方还各有一枚圆形棋子，称作"鱼"，将它们分别布于棋盘12曲格道上，两头当中名为"水"，"鱼"便置于

six pieces at the curved paths on their own sides. One of the pieces represented the "hero" (*Xiao*) which had privilege and the other five were the "scattered pieces" (*San*). During the game, the two sides took turns to throw the sticks and their moves were determined by the number of the sticks. The players would try to take their opponent's scattered pieces with the "hero", while moving around their own pieces to kill the opponent's "scattered pieces" at the right moment. When the "hero" was killed, the game was over.

During the Eastern Han Dynasty (25-220), the design of Liubo changed and Xiaobo (Lesser Bo) which was played with two dices (*Qiong*) was invented. One of the players would have six white pieces, while the other six black pieces. There was also a round piece for each player, known as the "fish". They would be placed at the twelve curved paths, which had two ends and an area of the "water" in the middle. The players would move their pieces based on the throw of the "dice", known as *Qiong*. When a piece had been moved to a certain place, it could stand up, and was called "*Jiaoqi*". Thereupon it could enter the "water" and eat the opponent's "fish", which was also called "pulling fish". Every time a player

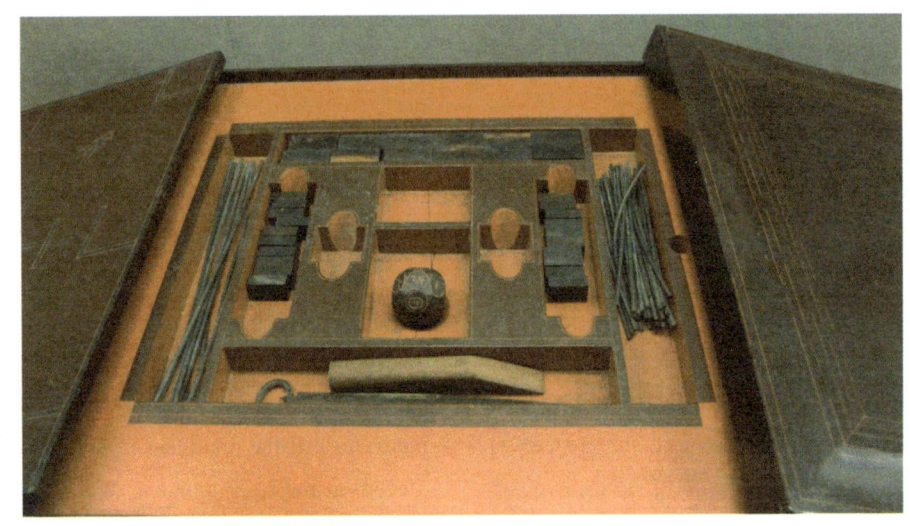

• 长沙马王堆汉墓出土的六博棋具
Liubo Equipment Unearthed from Mawangdui Tomb Built During the Han Dynasty (206 B.C.-220 A.D.) in Changsha City, Hunan Province

"水"中。行棋的多少是根据掷"茕"的数字决定，哪一枚棋子先进到规定的位置，即可竖起，称为"骄棋"。随后这枚"骄棋"便可入于"水"中，吃掉对方的"鱼"，称为"牵鱼"。每牵一次鱼，可获博筹两根，如能首先牵到三次鱼，得6根博筹，即算获胜。

pulled the fish he got two tokens, and if he pulled three fishes in a row he would win six tokens and the game was over.

> 塞戏

塞戏又称"簺戏""格五",诞生于春秋时期,盛行于汉代至南北朝时期,是从六博中衍生出来的一种棋戏。根据史籍的记载,塞戏从棋盘到玩法都与六博比较相近,区别是行棋时不用投箸,摆脱了侥幸取胜的成分。古籍中经常将其和六博以"博塞"并称。西汉王朝设有"棋待诏"的官衔。据《汉书》记载,汉武帝时的吾丘寿王就以擅长塞戏被召为"棋待诏"。《后汉书·梁冀传》中记载,东汉时的权臣梁冀也善"格五"。塞戏已经失传800多年,人们只能综合古籍片段,从中略知一二。东汉人边韶曾作《塞赋》咏塞戏:"始作塞者,其明哲乎。故其用物也约,其为乐也大。"就是说,发明塞戏的人肯

> Saixi

Saixi, also known as "Gewu", was invented in the Spring and Autumn Period (770 B.C.-476 B.C.) and became popular around the Han Dynasty (206 B.C.-220 A.D.) to the Southern and Northern dynasties (386-589). Saixi is a board game based on Liubo. According to the historical records, the board and rules of Saixi were very similar to that of Liubo. The only difference between the two games was that throwing sticks was not involved in playing *Saixi*, which avoided winning the game by chance. In ancient written works, Saixi and Liubo had been referred as "Bosai". In the Western Han Dynasty (206 B.C.-25 A.D.), there was an official title known as "board game attendant". According to *The History of the Han Dynasty*, Wuqiu Shouwang was recruited as a "board game attendant" for his skill in

定具有很深的智慧，所以塞戏所用的器具非常简单，却能给人带来乐趣。他在文中还描写了塞戏棋局的形制："本其规模，制作有式：四道交正，时之则也。"棋盘基本上为正方形，棋道相交。"棋有十二，律吕极也。人操厥半，六爻列也。赤白色者，分阴阳也。乍亡乍存，像日月也。"12枚棋子，每人6枚，像八卦中的重卦六爻一样，又按阴阳将棋分为红、白两色。行棋的过程忽盛忽衰，就像日月升落一样。

Saixi during the reign of Emperor Wu of the Han Dynasty. Besides, *Biography of Liangji* in *The History of Latter Han* mentioned that Liangji who was an important court official in the Eastern Han Dynasty was also good at playing "Gewu". Nevertheless, the rules of Saixi have been forgotten since over 800 years. Thus, we can only infer the rules from historical records. In the poem *Ode to Saixi* written by Bian Shao of the Eastern Han Dynasty, it says: "The inventor of Saixi must be a wise man. The equipment of Saixi is so simple, but it brings so much pleasure." It praises the wisdom of its inventor by using simple set for great pleasure. He also described the for formats of Saixi board: "The board of Saixi is regular. It has a square shape with crossed lines. Twelve pieces are used in the game. Each player has six pieces, which is similar to the six lines on a trigram of the double diagram in the Eight Diagrams. The pieces are also in two colors based on Yin-Yang Theory. The process of playing the game involves exciting and quite moments that like the rising and setting of the sun and the moon."

- 彩绘木俑塞戏（东汉）（图片提供：FOTOE）
这对塞戏木俑出土于甘肃武威磨嘴子汉墓。
Color Painted Wooden Figurines Playing Saixi (Eastern Han Dynasty, 25-220)
This pair of wood figurines was unearthed from the tomb built in the Han Dynasty (206 B.C.-220 A.D.) at Mozuizi, Wuwei City of Gansu Province.

> 弹棋

　　弹棋是西汉末年开始流行的一种棋戏，初创时主要流行于宫廷之中，在民间比较少见。西汉末年，天下大乱，各地农民起义不断，弹棋在乱世中从宫廷流入民间。到了东汉时期，喜好弹棋

- 彩绘漆奁（汉）
Painted Lacquer Toilet Box (Han Dynasty)

> Tanqi

Tanqi, a board game, was invented around the late Western Han Dynasty. Initially, it was only played in the royal palace. Because of the chaos in the country and numerous uprisings of farmers, Tanqi gradually spread to the ordinary people. In the Eastern Han Dynasty (25-220), it was liked by more and more people. Lots of literati wrote poems, proses, and papers about it, which promoted the development and spread of this game.

　　Tanqi was mentioned in *Miscellany of the Western Capital* written by Ge Hong of the Jin Dynasty (265-420). Besides, in *Records of Handicrafts* written by Handan Chun around the Three Kingdoms Period and the Jin Dynasty: "Tanqi was invented in the imperial court of the Kingdom of Wei (220-280). Inside the board, there is an

的人越来越多，文人纷纷为弹棋写诗作赋或撰文论述，推动了弹棋的普及和发展。

　　晋人葛洪的《西京杂记》中曾提到弹棋。魏晋时的邯郸淳在《艺经》中记载："弹棋，始自魏宫，内装器戏也。文帝于此技以特好。用手巾拂之，无不中。有客自云能，帝使为之。客著葛巾拂棋，妙逾于帝。"意思是说弹棋是始自魏朝宫廷，其内部装有器械。魏文帝曹丕十分擅长玩弹棋，用手巾来甩动，没有不击中的。有个人向文帝说自己也很擅长。文帝就请他来一试，客人拿下头上的头巾来击打弹棋，比文帝的技艺更精妙。所以也有人说弹棋是始于魏宫。

　　弹棋所用棋盘为正方形，中心隆起而四周低平，正如晚唐诗人李商隐诗中所说："玉作弹棋局，中心亦不平。"弹棋棋子一般为木质，也有石质或玉质。其玩法大致是二人对局，黑、白棋子各6枚，以自己的棋子击弹对方的棋子。由于棋盘中间隆起，若想击中对手，应该将自己的棋子弹过隆起的部分，使其从另一侧滑下去击中对方的棋

apparatus. Emperor Wen of the Wei State was good at playing this game. He would use his handkerchief to brush the pieces and could hit the goal every time. Once, someone said he could hit the goal every time, too. Emperor Wen thus invited him to come to the palace to play the game. The guest took off his headband and played the game even better than Emperor Wen." Therefore, the Kingdom of Wei was known as a potential origin of Tanqi.

　　Tanqi board is square with a raised section in the center and a flat rim. Li Shangyin of the late Tang Dynasty mentioned in his poem: "Tanqi pieces are made of jade. The centre of the board is not flat." Usually, Tanqi pieces were made of wood, but there were also stone and jade pieces. The general rule of Tanqi involves two players who either have six black or white pieces to hit the opponent's pieces with their own ones. As the centre of the board is raised, the players have to manipulate their pieces to pass this barrier and slid from the other side so as to hit the opponent's pieces. However, as the detailed rules of Tanqi cannot be found in written records, it is not clear how to play the game exactly.

　　The development of Tanqi reached

子。具体的对局方法，由于文献记载很少，目前还不是太清楚。

唐代是古代弹棋发展的一个高峰。诗人杜甫、白居易、李贺、韦应物等都留下不少以弹棋为主题的诗作。唐代的弹棋在棋型、布局和行棋步骤等方面，基本上因袭汉魏旧式，但也出现了一定的变革。棋局的形制，中间为圆顶，象征着天，局的四边代表地，与古代人天圆地方的观念相适。这样增加了弹棋的复杂性，因而在游戏方法上也发生了许多变化。唐代的棋子仍系木制或象牙雕刻而成，棋子的数量增至24枚。二人对局，每人12枚。每一方的12枚棋子中，又分贵子和贱子各6枚。唐代诗人柳宗元作《弹

- 唐代弹棋棋盘示意图
  Tanqi Board Used in the Tang Dynasty (618-907)

its peak in the Tang Dynasty (618-907). Many famous poets, including Du Fu, Bai Juyi, Li He, and Wei Yingwu wrote poems about Tanqi. The board, layout, and rules of Tanqi used in this period were similar to previous dynasties, but they included new forms. The board of Tanqi had a round top in the center to represent the sky, and the four rims of the board formed a square to symbolize the land. This format was consistent with ancient Chinese's concept of the universe that the sky is like a hemispherical dome and the land is like a flat square. Thus, the complexity of Tanqi had been increased and the rules of Tanqi included many variations accordingly. Tanqi pieces in the Tang Dynasty were also made of wood or carved from ivory. However, there were 24 instead of 12 pieces. In the game, each player would have 12 pieces. Among the 12 pieces, there were 6 superior ones and 6 inferior ones. In *Prologue of Tanqi* written by the poet Liu Zongyuan of the Tang Dynasty, it says: "There are 24 pieces. Half of them are superior ones and the other half are inferior ones. One shall use the inferior ones to attack the opponent's pieces one by one before using the superior ones." The pieces painted in black were inferior

棋序》说："置棋二十有四，贵者半，贱者半；贵曰上，贱曰下，咸自第一至十二。"涂以黑色为贱子，涂以红色的为贵子，玩时应先以己方贱子去击触对方的子，不得已才用贵子。可见，小小的弹棋成了等级社会的缩影。

到了宋代，也许是由于围棋、象棋特别兴盛，流行了几百年时间的弹棋不再流行，其玩法也从此失传了。

ones, while red ones were superior pieces. Superior ones could only be used after all the inferior ones failed to gain the points. Hence, the format of Tanqi reflected the life of the hierarchical society.

In the Song Dynasty (960-1279), with the increasing popularity of the game of Go and Chinese chess, Tanqi lost its popularity and its rules were gradually forgotten.

> 双陆

双陆是魏晋时期流行的一种棋类，于隋唐之际达到极盛，是一种模拟战场的游戏。

双陆最初是在贵族阶层流行起来的。《魏书·艺术传》记载，南北朝时狱中的犯人曾向当政者进献双陆。书中还记载了当时最著名的两位双陆高手——李幼序和丘何奴。《北史》中提到，北齐皇帝高湛甚至恩准大臣到后宫去和太后博双陆。双陆在南方也同样流行，据《南史》记载，梁元帝萧绎在即位之前做湘东王时就很喜欢下双陆棋。

到了隋唐以后，双陆真正走向了寻常百姓家。《隋唐嘉话》中记载，薛万彻是唐太宗麾下的一位宿将，太宗为酬其功，将女儿丹阳公

> Shuanglu

Shuanglu was a board game in the Three Kingdom Period and the Jin Dynasty. As a game simulates battlefield, it reached its zenith during the Sui and Tang dynasties.

Initially, Shuanglu gained popularity among the aristocrats. According to the *Records of Arts* in the *History of Wei*, a prisoner lived in the Southern and Northern dynasties (386-589) gave Shuanglu as a present for the rulers. The two most famous Shuanglu players, Li Youxu and Qiu Henu also earned their names in historical records. The *History of the Northern Dynasties* mentioned that Gao Zhan, the Emperor of the Northern Qi Dynasty even granted his court officials to play Shuanglu with his mother in the imperial residence. Shuanglu was also popular in the south. According to *History of the Southern Dynasties*, the Emperor Yuan of the Liang Dynasty,

主嫁给他。有一次，太宗见薛万彻武夫之气太盛，就说了句"薛驸马村气"。这句话很快就传到公主的耳朵里，气得她几个月不理薛万彻。太宗听说后，派人将夫妻二人

Xiao Yi was found of playing Shuanglu before he was enthroned.

In the Sui and Tang dynasties, Shuanglu was also played by ordinary people. According to *Anecdotes of the Sui and Tang Dynasties*, Emperor Taizong of

樗蒲

樗蒲是出现于汉末的一种棋类游戏。由于其游戏中用于掷采的骰子最初是用樗木制成，故而得名。樗蒲所用的骰子共有5枚，有黑有白，称为"五木"。它们可以组成六种不同的排列组合，也就是"六种彩"。其中全黑的称为"卢"，是最高彩；四黑一白的称为"雉"，仅次于卢；其余四种称为"枭"或"犊"，属于杂彩。游戏者在掷"五木"时往往喊叫希望得到"卢"，即所谓的"呼卢"。唐代玄宗年间，唐玄宗好樗蒲的游戏，权相杨国忠因善于樗蒲而大受宠幸。大诗人李白的名作《少年行》中也曾写道："呼卢百万终不惜，报仇千里如咫尺。"

Chupu

Chupu (literally, simarubaceae-calamus) is a board game that appeared in the late Han Dynasty. It was given this name, because the dices used in the game were initially made from simarubaceae. There are five black and white dices in total, known as "*Wumu*" (literally, five wood pieces). They can form six different permutations and combinations, known as "*Liuzhongcai*" (literally, six types of colors). If all of the dices are black ones, they are known as the most valuable "*Lu*"; Four black dices and one white dice are known as the less valuable "*Zhi*"; The rest four combinations are named "*Xiao*" or "*Du*", which are considered as miscellaneous colors. When the players threw the *Wumu* dices, they would shout out "*Lu*" loudly to express their desire to get it. This phenomenon was known as "calling *Lu*". During the reign of Emperor Xuanzong of the Tang Dynasty, Yang Guozhong, the powerful Prime Minister gained trust from the Emperor due to his skills in Chupu. In *A Young Man's Departure* written by the great poet Li Bai, he said: "One would not feel it was such a waste of money to spend over a million on gambling, but one would regard a thousand mile as a short distance if he desired a revenge."

叫来，当着公主的面和薛万彻下双陆棋，还以御用宝刀作为赌注。太宗在行棋中故意不敌，将宝刀输给了薛万彻。公主见夫婿得胜，感到自己有了面子，终于和薛万彻和好如初。唐人张鷟所辑《朝野佥载》

• 《内人双陆图》周昉（唐）【局部】
My Wives' Playing Shuanglu, by Zhou Fang (Tang Dynasty, 618-907) [Part]

the Tang Dynasty married his daughter Princess Danyang to his experienced veteran general named Xue Wanche. Once, the Emperor noticed that Xue was a bit rude and commented that "my son-in-law behaves so rustic". Princess Danyang was mad at Xue and ignored him for a few months after she got to know this incident shortly. When Emperor Taizong heard about this, he invited the couple to the palace one day. He played Shuanglu with Xue Wanche and used his royal sword as the stake in front of the Princess. Emperor Taizong lost the game deliberately so Xue Wanche won the sword. After seeing her husband won the game, the Princess found back her confidence and became reconciled with him. Besides, according to *Anecdotes form Court and Countryside* written by Zhang Zhuo of the Tang Dynasty, there was a Shuanglu fan named Pan Yan lived during the reign of the Emperor Gaozong of the Tang Dynasty. He took Shuanglu board with him wherever he travelled. Once, he encountered a shipwreck accident due to strong wind on the sea. He held bits of the ship with one hand, and Shuanglu board with the other. He even used his mouth to protect the game pieces and dices. After two consecutive

记载，唐高宗时期，有个叫潘彦的人对双陆非常痴迷，无论走到何处都会随身携带双陆。有一次他在海上遇风沉船，就一只手抓住一块船板，另一只手来拿双陆棋盘，棋子和骰子则含在嘴里。经过两天一夜的漂流，他终于漂到海岸。此时两只手已被海水浸得露出了骨头，但棋盘、棋子和骰子却完好无损。以上的故事从侧面反映了唐代初年双陆棋受欢迎的程度。

五代十国时期，双陆仍然在宫廷内大受欢迎。前蜀和后蜀两个政权都因偏安于四川，远离中原的战

days and a night, he finally reached the shore. Both of his hands were rotten away by sea water and one could see the bones, but the Shuanglu board, pieces, and dices were in impeccable condition. These two storied indirectly reflected the popularity of Shuanglu in the early Tang Dynasty.

During the the Five dynasties and Ten states (907-960), Shuanglu maintained its popularity in the imperial palace. For example, both the Earlier Shu State and the Later Shu State were located in relatively remote Sichuan Province and avoided the battles happening in the Central Plain at that time. Shuanglu became more popular in Sichuan compared with other places. In the Song Dynasty (960-1279), Shuanglu was still popular among all social classes. Emperor Huizong of the Northern Song Dynasty was not only an accomplished calligraphy artist and painter, but also a good player of Shuanglu. In his poems to describe life in the royal palace, he depicted the scenarios of his concubines' playing Shuanglu. Shuanglu was not only

• 下双陆图
Playing Shuanglu

乱，成为当时双陆的鼎盛之地。到了宋代，双陆依旧流行于各个社会阶层。北宋皇帝宋徽宗不仅是有成就的书画家，而且也是双陆行家，他御制的宫词中就曾多次描写过宫中嫔妃下双陆棋时的情态。双陆不仅在宫廷中大受欢迎，而且在酒肆中也很普及，人们可以边饮酒边玩双陆，甚至在瓦舍中双陆也是不可缺少的娱乐项目。南宋时，洪遵所著《谱双》是有关双陆的一部专著，后来被元代陶宗仪收入《说郛》一书中；清乾隆年间编修《四库全书》时，《说郛》又被收入其中。

在北方地区，双陆也广受欢迎。辽国的历代皇帝大都喜好双陆，他们与嫔妃博戏的事屡屡见于《辽史》《契丹国志》等史料中。据说掌辽国大权数十年的萧太后就经常与大臣韩德让下双陆棋，辽兴宗和胞弟耶律重元博双陆也有记载。

到了元代，双陆继续流行，《元史》中就有元顺帝和宠臣麻哈下双陆棋的记载。在当时流行的杂剧、散曲中，有关双陆的内容也频频出现。如杂剧大家关汉卿的代表

popular in the royal palace, but also in the folk society. In taverns, customers would play Shuanglu while having alcohol. Shuanglu was an indispensable entertainment activity even in *Washe* (Entertainment venues) In the Southern Song Dynasty (1127-1279), Hong Zun wrote a book about Shuanglu named *Variants of Shuanglu.* Later, Tao Zongyi lived in the Yuan Dynasty included this book when he compiled *Shuo Fu.* During the reign of Emperor Qianlong of the Qing Dynasty, *Shuo Fu* was then compiled in the *Complete Library in the Four Branches of Literature.*

Shuanglu was also popular in the northern areas. All the emperors of the Liao Dynasty (907-1125) liked playing Shuanglu. Many historical records, including *History of the Liao Dynasty* and *History of Khitan* mentioned about them playing Shuanglu with their concubines. It was said that the Empress Dowager Xiao who had been in charge of the regime for over ten years often played Shuanglu with the court official named Han Derang. In historical records, Emperor Xingzong of the Liao Dynasty played Shuanglu with his younger brother Yelü Chongyuan.

In the Yuan Dynasty (1206-1368),

• 新疆阿斯塔纳墓地出土的唐代双陆棋盘（图片提供：FOTOE）
Shuanglu Board of the Tang Dynasty (618-907) Unearthed from the Astara Tomb in Xinjiang Uygur Autonomous Region

作《一枝花·不伏老》中就有"我也会围棋、会蹴鞠、会打围、会插科、会歌舞、会吹弹、会咽作、会吟诗、会双陆"的长句，将双陆与围棋、蹴鞠、歌舞这些当时流行的娱乐活动相提并论，可见其普及的程度。

随着元代海外贸易的繁盛，双陆随着中国商船传入南洋及阿拉伯等地，进而在整个亚洲流传开来。

至明代，双陆经过不断改进，

Shuanglu maintained its popularity. According to *History of the Yuan Dynasty*, Emperor Shun of the Yuan Dynasty played Shuanglu with his favorite court official named Maha. Shuanglu was also frequently mentioned in popular miscellany plays and literary songs. For example, in the great play writer Guan Hanqing's works *I am not an Old Man with the format of One Flower*, he said in a long verse that "I know how to play Go, kick ball, sing opera arias,

与唐代的规则已大相径庭。在明代世情小说《金瓶梅》中，说起哪个人多才多艺，必定会说他"会打一

• **粉彩山水图双陆樽（清）**
双陆樽因形制仿古代"双陆"棋子的器型而得名，是清代雍正时期极具特色的一种瓷器造型。

Pastel Colored Rose Porcelain Shuanglu Vase with Landscape Painting (Qing Dynasty, 1616-1911)

The Shuanglu vase is known for having similar shape to the "Shuanglu" piece in ancient times. It is a unique porcelain shape produced during the reign of Emperor Yongzheng (1723-1735) of the Qing Dynasty.

act funny, dance, play several musical instruments, sing, make poem, and play Shuanglu". The use of Shuanglu together with Go, ball kicking, and dance as examples of popular entertainment activities at that time showed the popularity of Shuanglu.

With the prosperity of overseas trade in the Yuan Dynasty (1206-1368), Shuanglu spread to Southeast Asia and Arabic areas, and then the whole Asia.

In the Ming Dynasty (1368-1644), the rules of Shuanglu were different from the ones used in the Tang Dynasty (618-907). In *Jinpingmei* (*Golden Lotus*), a novel written in the Ming Dynasty would use "playing Shuanglu well" to describe versatile men, which showed the popularity of Shuanglu back then. At the end of the Ming Dynasty, fewer records of Shuanglu were found and the game was almost forgotten in the middle of the Qing Dynasty.

As Shuanglu had been widely popular for a long time, different places and time periods had different rules. The most popular one was known as "Northern Shuanglu" with a wooden rectangle board. The board was divided into two sections, with 12 routes on each side, known as "Beam". 6 beams were in

手好双陆",可见双陆在当时流行的程度。明代末年,关于双陆的记载渐渐变少,到清代中期双陆已基本失传。

在玩法方面,由于双陆流行时间长且范围广,所以不同地区、不同年代的双陆多有不同。通行的双陆为"北双陆",棋盘为木制,长方形。全局分左右两边,每边各十二路,叫"梁",前、后各分六梁。棋子称为"马",其形状为上粗下细的棒槌形,分黑、白两种,

the front, while the other 6 were in the back. The pieces were made of wood and known as "Horse". They were thick on one end and thin on the other, thus they looked like wooden clubs. The black pieces were known as "black horses" and white ones as "white horses". Each player would have fifteen pieces. Five pieces were initially placed on the sixth beam at the right side, and five pieces on the first beam at the left back side. Two pieces on the sixth beam at the right back side, and three pieces on the second beam at

• **紫檀双陆棋盘与棋子** (图片提供:FOTOE)
Red Sandalwood Shuanglu Board and Pieces

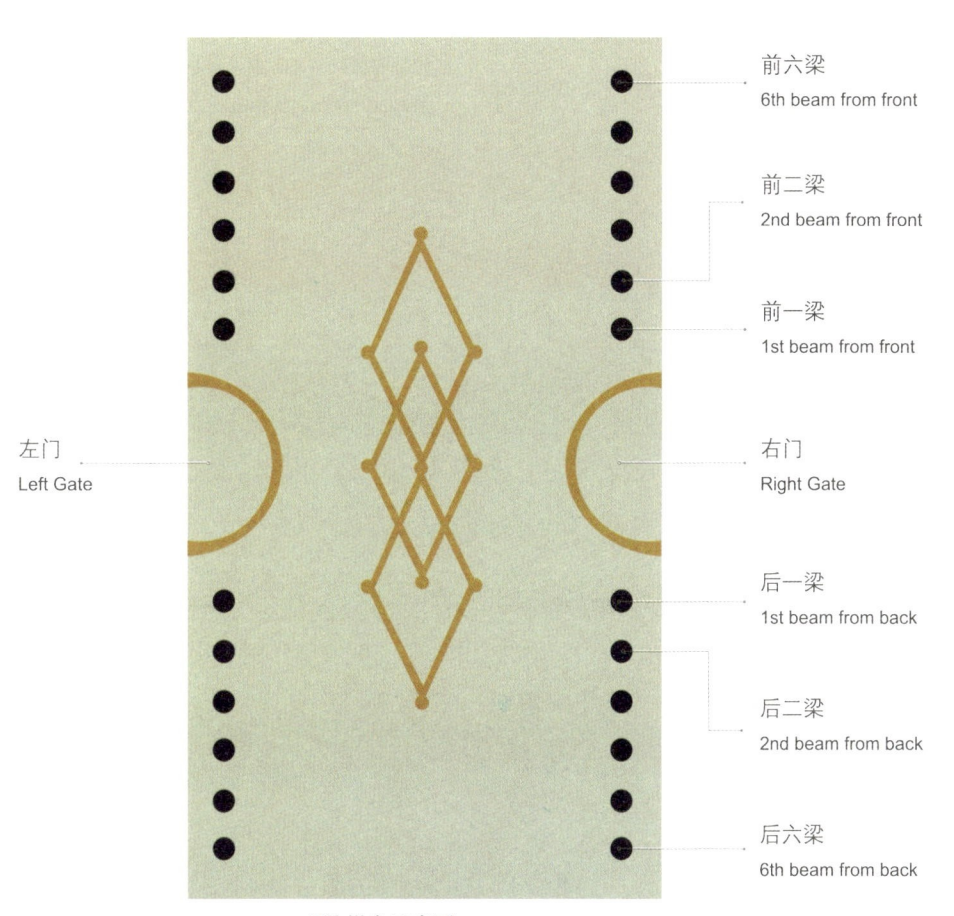

	前六梁 6th beam from front
	前二梁 2nd beam from front
	前一梁 1st beam from front
左门 Left Gate	右门 Right Gate
	后一梁 1st beam from back
	后二梁 2nd beam from back
	后六梁 6th beam from back

• 双陆棋盘示意图
Diagram of Shuanglu Board

白色的为白马，黑色的为黑马；各十五子，均为木制。双方开始的布子方式为右前六梁、左后一梁各五子，右后六梁二子，左前二梁三子。执白马者居右，执黑马者居左。二人对坐，用两枚骰子掷骰行马，最终以马先出尽者为胜。

the left front side. The player with white pieces would play on the right side, while the player with black pieces on the left side. The players sat opposite to each other. They move around the pieces by the roll of two dices. When the player played all of his pieces, he won the game.

> 蒙古象棋

蒙古象棋，蒙古语称为"沙塔拉"，又写作"喜塔尔"，是流行于蒙古族民间的一种棋。

早在北方草原契丹王朝时期就有关于沙塔拉（蒙古象棋）游戏的记载，不过当时的棋子和着法比现在的蒙古象棋简单一些。相传在成吉思汗西征时，蒙古象棋开始在民间流传，形成了独具特色的走法，成为一种智慧游戏。明朝永乐年间的《艺仙集》有关蒙古象棋的记载表明，现代蒙古象棋的走法早在14世纪末已定型。直到清代《口北三厅志》转引明人的《艺仙集》介绍蒙古象棋的走法及规则，这种古老的棋类才开始为更多人所知。清代叶明澧的《桥西杂记》曾录有关于当时蒙古象棋的文字："局纵横九

> Mongolian Chess

Mongolian chess is known as "Shatar" and "Hiashatar" in Mongolian.

As early as the Khitan Dynasty in Northern Prairie, there were records about Shatar (Mongolian chess), but back then it was played with relatively plain pieces and easier rules compared with the modern Mongolian chess. Legend has that during Genghis Khan's western expedition. Monglian chess began to circulate among the ordinary people and formed a unique way of moving, becoming a game of wisdow. According to *Yi Xian Ji* written during Yongle Period of the Ming Dynasty (1368-1644), the modern Mongolian chess formed its rules in the 14th century. It was more known by the public in the Qing Dynasty (1616-1911) after the book *Records of Three Bureaus North of Zhangjiakou* cited the form and rules of Mongolian

● 铜质蒙古象棋（图片提供：微图）
Mongolian Chess Set Made of Copper

线，六十四罫（盘中的方格）。棋各十六枚：八卒、二车、二马、二象、一炮、一将，别以朱墨，将居中之右，炮居中之左，车、马、象左右列，卒横于前。棋局无河界，满局可行，所谓随水草以为畜牧也。"

现在的蒙古象棋的某些走法与国际象棋相同，同时又保留着自己的特色。它的棋盘和国际象棋的棋盘一样是正方形，由深、浅两色交替排列的64个小方格组成。浅色的称白格，深色的称黑格。棋子也分白、黑两种，共32个，双方各有一王（称为"诺颜"，意即"首领"）、一帅、双车、双驼、

chess from *Yi Xian Ji*. The *Miscellanea of the West Bridge* written by Ye Mingli of the Qing Dynasty mentioned about the Mongolian chess: "Nine vertical lines and nine horizontal lines form sixty-four checks on the board. There are sixteen game pieces, including eight Pawns, two Chariots, two Horses, two Elephants, one Cannon, and one Lord. The two sides are distinguished by red and black colors. The Lord would be in the middle, the Cannon on the left, Chariots, Horses, and Elephants on both sides, Pawns in the front. There is no border on the board, and thus the pieces can move around freely, known as breeding the cattle at the right place."

Modern Mongolian chess have some

• 骨质蒙古象棋（图片提供：微图）
Mongolian Chess Set Made of Bones

双马和八个小兵。和国际象棋一样，蒙古象棋的棋子也是雕刻的立体造型，但把"象"刻成骆驼形，"兵"则是猎狗的形象，带有蒙古族游牧生活的特点。

similar rules to chess, but it has its own features. For example, similar to chess, Mongolian chess has the square board with 64 small checks painted in two shades. Checks with the shallow color are known as white checks, while deep color ones are black checks. The 32 game pieces are also in black and white colors. Each side has a Lord (known as Nuoyan, the leader), a General, two Chariots, two Camels, two Horses, and eight Pawns. Similar to chess, Mongolian chess pieces are also carved as solid pieces, while "Elephants" are replaced with camels and "pawns" are hounds, which reveals the characteristics of nomadic life of Mongolian people.

> 藏棋

藏棋是流行于中国藏族聚居地区的棋类游戏，包括"密芒"和"久"两大类别。

"密芒"又叫"多眼棋""多目戏"，实际上是由古代围棋演变而来的，和围棋的着法和提子方面的规则十分相近。另外，对局一开始就要在棋盘上预先按固定的位置各放6枚棋子，称为"座子"，这实际上也是保留了古代围棋的规则。

关于"密芒"在西藏的起源，有人认为其出现于汉代，由居住在四川、青海一带的古羌族人传入西藏；也有人说藏棋源于古印度；还有人认为藏棋是由三国时期的蜀汉丞相诸葛亮带入云南地区，又从云南传入西藏的。一般认为第一种和第三种的可能性较大。

> Tibetan Board Games

Tibetan board games are played in the areas inhabited by Tibetan, which can be categorized into "Mimang" and "Jiu".

"Mimang", also known as "Multiple Eyes Game" and "Several Eyes Game", is developed based on the ancient Go. Thus, it shares similar rules with Go in terms of moving and capturing the game pieces. Besides, at the beginning of the game, six pieces will be placed on fixed positions as the "basic pieces", which preserves the rules of ancient Go.

There are no consistent views about how "Mimang" spread to Tibet. Some believe that this game was introduced to Tibet by the ancient Qiang people from the Sichuan and Qinghai areas in the Han Dynasty (206 B.C.-220 A.D.). Some others argue that this game originated in ancient India. Others speculate that this game was brought to Yunnan areas by

密芒古代大多在藏族的统治阶层中流行。敦煌文献有记载，吐蕃时期有位大臣叫琼布·苏孜色，不仅政治和军事才能出众，而且善下密芒，棋艺高超，还能边处理公事边下棋。公元17世纪前后，密芒的发展进入兴盛时期，当时在西藏、青海、四川、甘肃、云南等地都出现了不少密芒高手。后来，密芒逐渐演变为上层贵族和寺庙僧侣的游戏，脱离了下层百姓，逐渐衰落。

藏棋棋盘纵横各17道，对局前12个子要先摆放好，黑子与白子各6个，执白者先走。藏棋一大奇特之处是，既可以两人对下，也可以4人或6人对下。下棋没有时间限制，一般要三四个小时才能下完一局。

"久"主要流行于青海的海南和青南地区，其棋盘的种类很多，如鱼棋、狼和羊棋、国王和大臣棋等，下法也与围棋截然不同。最特别的是，"久"胜负判定的必要条件不是吃掉对方多少棋子或占了多少面积，而是必须在棋盘上摆出一些固定的棋形。

- 藏族民居（图片提供：微图）
  Tibetan Dwellings

Zhuge Liang, the Prime Minister of the Kingdom of Shu-Han (221-263) in the Three Kingdoms Period (220-280), and then spread to Tibet from Yunnan. Most people regard the first and third sayings as more creditable.

In ancient times, Mimang was popular among the Tibetan ruling class. According to historical records from Dunhuang, In the Tubo Kingdom, there was a court official called Kyung po spungs sad zu tse who was not only renowned for his political and military talents, but also excellent skills in Mimang. He could even work while playing Mimang. Around the 17th century, Mimang reached its peak in its development. Back then, many good players of Mimang were from Tibet,

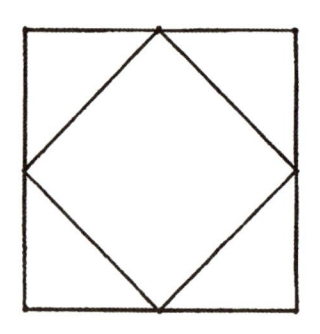

• 鱼棋
Fish Chess Board

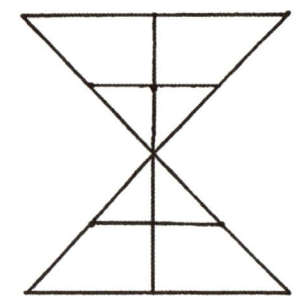

• 狼和羊棋
Wolf and Sheep Chess Board

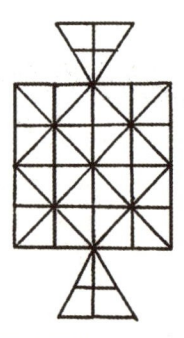

• 国王和大臣棋
King and Court Officials Chess Board

Qinghai, Sichuan, Gansu, and Yunnan, etc. Later, Mimang was only played by aristocrats and monks, thus it gradually declined because it was distant from the general public.

There are 17 vertical lines and 17 horizontal lines on the board. Before the game starts, 12 pieces would be placed on the board, including 6 black pieces and 6 white pieces. White makes the first move. There is a unique feature of this game: it can be played by two persons, but it can also be played by four or six persons at the same time. As there is no time limit, it often takes three to four hours to finish one game.

The game "Jiu" is mainly played in Hainan and Qingnan areas of Qinghai Province. There are a variety of board games, including Yu Qi (Fish), the Wolf and Sheep chess, and the King and Court Officials chess, etc. The rules involving these boards are also quite different. There is a unique way of "Jiu" to decide the winner: Necessary condition to win the game does not depend on the number of prisoners from the opponent side and the area of occupied territory, but the patterns that the players are able to arrange with their pieces.

> 鄂伦春围棋

鄂伦春族主要分布在内蒙古及黑龙江等省区。鄂伦春围棋称为"斑代"，是鄂伦春族传统的棋类，是在桦树皮上画上棋盘，棋子

> Oroqen Board Game

The Oroqen people mainly live in Inner Mongolia and Heilongjiang. The Oroqen Board Game, named "Bandai", is a traditional game played by the Oroqen people. The board is painted on the skin

• 头戴狍皮帽的鄂伦春人
Oroqen Wearing Roe Deer Hats

为三角形小木块制成。下棋时一方持24个小三角木块作为兵卒，另一方持两个大三角形木块为猛兽。双方先在棋盘上按照固定的阵势摆好棋子：持小木块的一方在棋盘的8个交叉点先布上8个子，持大木块的一方则把子布在棋盘两端的交叉处。持大子的一方先走，要设法吃掉小子，但必须跳一格才能吃。小子需要把格堵死，不让大子跳吃。大子每走一步，小子可布一子，如大子一方被小子围得寸步难行，即为小子一方获胜；如果小子一方的兵力被大子吃得不足以包围大子，即为大子一方获胜。

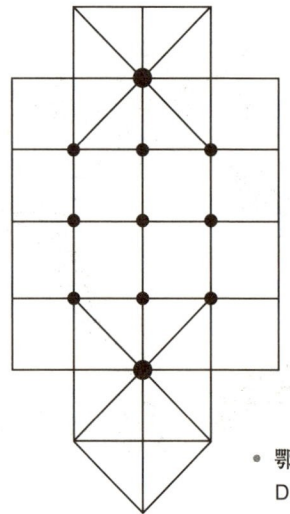

of birch and the game pieces are made of small chunks of wood in the triangle shape. One player has 24 small triangular pieces as Pawns, while the other has two big triangular pieces as Monsters. The two players put their pieces at fixed positions on the board. The player with small pieces places eight of them at the eight intersections in the center, while the player with big pieces places his pieces at the intersections on the corners of the board. The big pieces make first move and will try to eat nearby small pieces if there is an empty intersection between them. The small pieces will try to fill in the intersections so as to avoid being captured. After every move of the big piece, one small piece can be placed on the board. When the big pieces are encircled by the small pieces and cannot make any further moves, the player with small pieces wins the game. When the small pieces are incapable of encircling the big pieces due to the loss of Pawns, the player with big pieces wins the game.

● 鄂伦春围棋示意图
Diagram of the Oroqen Board Game